LEADING WITH AWARENESS

T0334422

Presenting the essentials of awakened leadership through 50 contemplative branches, this text is a revolutionary yet sensible leadership manual that takes the reader from self-reflection to interaction, touching on internal and external factors that influence business decision-making.

This book is designed to expand awareness within those who lead at present or those who aspire to lead. One can only lead others responsibly having understood how to lead the self, becoming an "awakened leader." Awakened leaders stay true to their values but are very much aware that life and business are continuous processes of growth and change—an awareness more critical than ever in today's VUCA world. Awakened leaders recognize that these constant changes are calls to regular reflection, enabling greater empathy, understanding, and ultimately, improved decision-making.

Postgraduate students and practicing leaders in the workplace will value this book, which tells them in a straightforward way how to undertake no-nonsense action with a compassionate and visionary foundation.

Joan Marques reinvented herself from entrepreneur to edupreneur, currently serving as Dean, School of Business, Woodbury University in Burbank, CA. She (co-)authored/edited more than 31 books so far. She lives, teaches, and writes about awakened leadership within a spiritual context.

LEADING WITH AWARENESS

A Roadmap for Awakened Leaders

Joan Marques

Routledge
Taylor & Francis Group

NEW YORK AND LONDON

First published 2021
by Routledge
605 Third Avenue, New York, NY 10158

and by Routledge
2 Park Square, Milton Park, Abingdon, Oxon, OX14 4RN

Routledge is an imprint of the Taylor & Francis Group, an informa business

Library of Congress Cataloging-in-Publication Data
Names: Marques, Joan, author.
Title: Leading with awareness : a roadmap for awakened leaders /
    Joan Marques.
Description: New York, NY : Routledge, 2021. | Includes
    bibliographical references and index.
Subjects: LCSH: Leadership.
Classification: LCC HM1261 .M37 2021 (print) | LCC HM1261
    (ebook) | DDC 303.3/4—dc23
LC record available at https://lccn.loc.gov/2021003241
LC ebook record available at https://lccn.loc.gov/2021003242

ISBN: 978-0-367-89628-7 (hbk)
ISBN: 978-0-367-89399-6 (pbk)
ISBN: 978-1-003-02017-2 (ebk)

Typeset in Bembo
by Apex CoVantage, LLC

CONTENTS

PREFACE

Leading With Awareness provides those who aspire leadership positions a manual that they can read in any order they prefer. While the book will have its highest impact when read from beginning to end, there will not be an understanding barrier if you simply open the work at any section and start reading there. This book presents "awakened leadership" essentials through 50 contemplative branches—rather than conventional chapters—entailing the most important reflections, considerations, and behavioral gems.

The name "Awakened Leader" was inspired by a story of Gautama Siddhartha's enlightenment, which got him to be known as "the Buddha" (the awakened one) afterward. Upon a lengthy insight meditation, Siddhartha was walking up a road, when he encountered a passerby, who was stunned by his radiance and asked him whether he was a wizard, a God, or some other kind of other super-being. The Buddha simply responded that he was "awake." Being an awakened leader entails being mindful, and acquiring a deep understanding of what really matters. Awakened leaders remain authentic and true to their values at all times, but also realize that they were not born with all the answers and that life is a continuous process of growth and change. Awakened leaders are very aware of their flaws as human beings, and the continuous need to assess their practices. They are very much shaped by occurrences in their lives. These occurrences differ from one individual to another, yet they consistently pave the road to wakefulness for all who seek it. Life's occurrences incite two important qualities: reflection and empathy. In the course of their path to maturity, awakened leaders may have faced issues that caused them to question their morals and reflect on the need to possibly reconsider them. Where needed, they did so, in the understanding that people, situations, and insights change, and that regular reflection can be an eye-opening path toward greater empathy and understanding, and hence, more responsible decision-making. *Leading With Awareness* will take you from self-reflective explorations to interactive aspects, as well as external factors that influence insights and decision-making.

Through years of leadership studies and observations, it has become apparent to me, the author, that leading others responsibly is only possible if you lead yourself responsibly. No one wants to follow a leader who makes repeated and inconsiderate blunders in his or her actions. Unfortunately, workplaces are filled with those types of individuals in leading positions, but the conscious question we can ask ourselves here is: "Are these people leaders or do they just fulfill these positions in a poor way?"

In order to be accepted as someone else's leader, you don't have to hold a formal leadership position, but you will have to profile a strong, authentic, admirable set of behaviors and reasoning. Thus, in the depictions developed to clarify the structure of this work, it may become clear that a fundamental aspect of leading lies in the will to reflect, which entails turning inward, and exploring one's values, beliefs, and motives.

Aimed at workforce members and adult learners, each of the "tidbits" or "branches" in this work consists of a blend of theory (only where appropriate), reflective examples, stories, and other literary tools to enhance the appeal and clarity of the material.

The foundational section of this book presents a reflective take on the questions one should ask before stepping into a leader role. At this point, it is also critical, given our fast-paced, interconnected, and challenging world, to explore one's purpose, potential problems, and initial perspectives on how to solve these from a macro viewpoint.

Following the internal exploration process, the work will deliberate on a variety of aspects that leaders should consider and utilize as behavioral guides on a regular basis. In order to do so, this book will be one that leaders should keep at hand, in order to glance regularly through it after the first read, in order to renew insights, good intentions, and a focus on the righteous path in decision making.

I wish you a joyful reading experience!

Joan Marques

PART I
Self-Inspection

1

AM I A LEADER?

THE LEADER INSIDE

This path I am treading
Is paved by the choices I made
And will evolve as a result
Of how through life I wade

While the world outside
May influence the tide
My perspectives and actions
Make my path narrow or wide

I may not be in charge
Of whatever might emerge
But my attitude guides me
In converting drought to surge

The leader of my life
I am, without a doubt
I'm grateful for my steps
In living good, gentle, yet stout

~ *Joan Marques*

Are you a leader? Not sure if you ever asked yourself this question, but chances are that the answer varies based on the circumstances. If you're down and out, or just had a major disappointment, you most likely think that you are definitely not leader material. On the other hand, if you just graduated, landed a great job, received a promotion, or had your partner agree to your marriage proposal you may give yourself a pat on the back as a remarkable leader.

And indeed, it depends, but in a different way than described previously. If you consider being a leader something like holding a formal position of authority over others, you may not meet your own criteria. But if you agree that leadership starts within, and manifests itself through your behavior and actions, you have a high chance of making the leadership ranks.

One favorite thought I heard some time ago is that we're all born leaders, because we are the one sperm that managed to break through the barrier of an egg cell and fertilize it. Perceived that way, each of us is a winner and could see themselves as a leader. But most people don't think of leadership as a set of behaviors. They consider it positional, and that is a misnomer, because there have been numerous people who held great formal positions, and were worthless as leaders. Similarly, there were, and still are, many people in the simplest of positions—or even without jobs—who carry themselves in such a way that others gravitate to them for advice and to hear their opinion. Those people have more leadership qualities in their pinky fingers than the ones holding major positions, but are narcissistic and inconsiderate toward others.

Leadership is the way you carry yourself. It is displayed through your focus and your grit. Grit is something that cannot be taught. It's that inner desire to succeed at something you consider important, and that propels you forth long after others have given up. That's grit. And that's one of the remarkable qualities of true leaders.

Another critical factor that can help you determine if you are a leader is your driving motives: Do you only focus on your own progress, or do you have a sense of responsibility toward those around you? Whether this pertains to coworkers, family members, or pets, we all find ourselves in a position where we have to take care of others. This may not always be a desirable place to be, but if you are able to take on that responsibility for others, aside from yourself, and make something good of it, you may label yourself a leader.

In fact, no one said that leadership is fun. Sometimes the pressure of taking on leadership is downright hard. Whether this pertains to leadership over your own actions and decisions or those of others. This may explain why so many people actually prefer not to consider themselves leaders: it's not easy. Leadership is not only responsibility but also care, insight, awareness, and setting a good example for others. That takes off a large chunk of the fun in life, because as a leader, you should keep in mind that others will want to follow your example. So, what example are you setting?

2

WHY SHOULD I BE A LEADER?

For the longest time, I thought that everyone would like to be a leader. Over the years I asked this question to undergraduate and MBA business students, and I became aware that this is not the case. In fact, a majority of the people I asked whether they saw themselves as a leader responded negatively to this question. Many of them did not even consider it viable that they would be a leader anytime soon in their lives.

I started understanding that this mindset may have originated from what is generally being taught, namely, that you are only a leader when you hold a formal leadership position. More narrowly defined: many people think that they would only be a leader if they were the CEO of a corporation. This, in my opinion, is a misleading notion. Why? Because we exert leadership all the time! Deciding to do this and not that is a leadership task. Any decision we make ultimately influences the course of our path from here to the future. Now, is that not leadership, then?

Reflecting on the title of this section, the answer could therefore easily be: you should be a leader because you already are, whether you like it or not. The difference, from the moment the awareness of your self-leadership kicks in, is that you also get an increased understanding of the responsibility you have for your actions, and the fact that a large part of your fate lies in your own hands. While you cannot change certain circumstances, you can change what you do when the circumstances emerge. If, for instance, you have lost a job, relationship, or an opportunity you had hoped for, this may get you down and in despair. Such emotions are understandable, and you should take the time to mourn the sense of loss you feel. Yet, you cannot do this forever. At some point you will have to get up, straighten your shoulders, take a deep breath, and bounce back!

Bouncing back. We may not have the literal buoyancy of a rubber ball, but if you had no resilience at all, you probably wouldn't have been able to read this book at this moment, and if I did not have any, I wouldn't have been able to write it.

Resilience is a powerful self-leadership trait that enables us to withstand more than we would ever hold possible. Do you know the story of the professor and the jar, filled with rocks? When he asked his students if they considered the jar full, the students admitted that this was the case. Immediately, the professor proved them wrong by pouring fine sand in the jar. The sand trickled down and nestled itself in the spaces between the rocks. The professor asked the students if the jar was full now, and again the students agreed, upon which the professor poured some water in the jar, demonstrating that there was still some holding capacity in the jar.

This little story can be interpreted in many positive ways, but it definitely illustrates the power of resilience. If we compare ourselves to the jar, we can understand our capacity to overcome more challenges than we might have initially thought we could. There is oftentimes just a little more capacity than we thought ourselves to have. It's the resilient leadership in us that creates enough elasticity to go yet another mile, in the meantime getting over mental wounds we thought would never heal.

Our human frailty is rather deceptive, because in reality, we are capable of so much more. Resilience ties in well with perseverance and persistence. Actually, if there were any family ties possible between words, these three could be siblings. All of them represent strength and endurance to a level that could be decisive for the quality of our lives.

Now, you may wonder: what is it that makes some people more resilient, thus driven, than others? Is it an inborn trait or can it be learned? Several scholars have done research on this topic, and they agreed that resilience can be learned, so we all can increase our level of resilience if we choose to. With resilience comes a greater sense of responsibility, as mentioned earlier: you understand that you cannot point fingers at others for the things that go wrong in your life, because you are ultimately the one who made the decisions to be in the here and now.

Resilient people have a tendency to take a hard look at themselves, assess where they may have gone wrong in order to have landed in the current situation, and how they could elevate themselves to better conditions.

That is the exertion of leadership, directed at self-improvement. If you get in the habit of implementing this, you will soon find yourself in positions of formal leadership, because others will start recognizing your qualities, and want you to apply them to their environments as well.

3

WHO BENEFITS FROM ME BEING A LEADER?

This is one of those many questions that is best answered with, "It depends." Answering the question this way is not a means to avoid a straight answer. It is just the truth. The type of leader you choose to be will determine whether anyone—including yourself—will benefit from it or not. The factors that this depends on are not only limited to your behavior, by the way, but they also depend on the environment involved. Sometimes there are a large number of stakeholders involved in, let's say, a corporate or academic environment where you fulfill a formal leadership role, and sometimes there may only be a small group of individuals involved. Either way: it is important to reflect regularly on this important question: "who benefits from me being a leader?"

Without intending for the following to sound self-centered, you should try to discover some personal benefits from leading. Not just the financial reward that so often comes with a leadership position and not just the influence you will be able to exert toward certain groups. Leadership is a great opportunity to learn about yourself and to develop skills that you discover toward improvement. If, for instance, you find that you are highly sensitive about what others say about you, you may have to work on that, because you will not escape the fact that not everyone will be equally fond of you. Some people may respect you, but dislike some of your traits or the way you look or talk. Others may feel just the opposite: they may like how you look or present yourself, but they don't respect you as a leader. And in between there are numerous shades of opinions.

That's why it is important to reflect and see things in perspective. People include their biases and experiences in the pictures they paint of others, and their opinions about you may be tainted by the mental lenses they wear. This is why you have to practice the art of emotionally releasing when you find yourself hurt due to misinterpretations or biased views. If performing in any leadership role is too painful and stressful and undermines your well-being, you should consider bringing about some drastic changes, either by shifting your perspectives or by changing your environment.

Reflecting is also useful as a tool to mentally scan the entire landscape in which you perform. Regardless of your ideas about anyone you encounter in your leadership practice, you should always try to do your very best to help. And whenever you cannot help, try to refrain from harming. This is an old Buddhist concept, but it works in any situation, and it is morally responsible as well.

Leadership can sometimes come across as a thankless job. You may find yourself trying to accomplish so much for those you serve as a leader, yet, they complain and speak poorly about you whenever they can. At any rate, you have to remain devoted to your conscience, and try to maintain a broad view on your role: to serve your stakeholders and the organization you represent, and to do so, with the best intentions, even though outcomes and opinions may not reflect your efforts.

Sometimes it takes many years for people to realize how you benefitted them with your leadership efforts. That's okay. Some people may never realize it. That's okay too. As long as your intentions and efforts are morally sound, and you can distill growth for yourself and others in the process, you are on the right track.

PART II

What's My Purpose?

4

UNDERSTANDING

"Seek first to understand and then to be understood." That's what Stephen Covey (1990) teaches us in his all-time bestselling book, *The Seven Habits of Highly Effective People*. And I am sure that this recommendation is not limited to just that book and that management guru. It's actually a very basic and wise statement: the foundation of any successful cooperation between two or more entities.

In management, whether career or life management, understanding is an invaluable skill and a powerful tool. If you develop the habit to at least try to understand where others come from in their reasoning, any argument or conflict becomes unnecessary. Trying to understand others doesn't mean that you also have to agree with their point of view. Yet, it establishes mutual respect and goodwill. When your discussion partner senses that you are making an attempt to know where he or she comes from, this person will get inspired to do the same. And what turns a "discussion" more easily into a "dialogue" than this positive attitude? Remember, there's a significant difference between discussion and dialogue. The word "discussion" holds a somewhat violent character, stemming from "discus," which is a disk, typically wooden or plastic, with a metal rim that is thrown for distance in athletic competitions. Discussion itself is defined in Dictionary.com as "the act of discussing or exchanging reasons; examination by argument; debate; disputation; agitation." See the word lineup there? Nothing peaceful or serene about that, isn't it? On the other hand, the same source describes "dialogue" as "a conversation between two or more people" or "an exchange of ideas or opinions."

It is, then, easy to deduce that mutual attempts toward understanding can change a discussion into a dialogue; can change competition into cooperation; can change win–lose into win–win situations. And no, those are not idealistic platitudes. They are as real as their negative precursors, which we usually take for granted.

Demonstrating a desire to understand others has a positive effect on an existing atmosphere. Even if it may remain difficult to comprehend where others are coming from, or to muster sympathy for their viewpoints, it is the effort that may disarm senses of antagonism between parties. But trying to understand also does something good to you internally. It triggers an inner sense of respect for the other party, and a will to get closer rather than distance yourself.

The first step toward developing the ability to understand the other party is to realize that we all have our own reality, colored by our history, culture, and personality. No two realities are the same. The way you see the world is not the same as how your friend, colleague, or business partner, sees it. The reason is simply, that you see things through your personal interpretation, which has been shaped by your upbringing, environment, culture, believes, and so on. And what goes for you goes for others as well.

The above represents the basic reason for differences in opinion and perception. Once you understand that perception varies from one individual to another, due to the factors just mentioned, you'll also realize that what the other party is saying or doing is making perfect sense to them from their point of view, and that this person wonders just as much as you why you are giving them such a hard time! This must have been the reasoning behind Carl Jung's statement, "If one does not understand a person, one tends to regard him as a fool" (Jung, N/A).

Yet, the statement from Jung also clarifies how we tend to label those with whom we cannot associate: rather than considering that *we* have a shortcoming by being unable to understand their stance, we fail to question ourselves and throw all the blame of foolishness on them.

The will to understand others can have an astoundingly positive impact on every relationship; it also creates serenity within the person who seeks to achieve it. The power of understanding can also be explained through the following cycle: The will to understand enhances the will to be understood, which improves mutual understanding, establishes unity in perception, increases power, leading to influence, respect, and appreciation.

References

Covey, S. (1990). *The Seven Habits of Highly Effective People*. Simon & Schuster Trade, Avon, MA.

Jung, C. (N/A). If one does not understand a person . . . *Goodreads.com*. Retrieved from www. goodreads.com/quotes/198003-if-one-does-not-understand-a-person-one-tends-to.

5

CONTENTMENT

We all have that special place within us: a source that could be regarded as the creator or stimulator of all our achievements. Unfortunately, not all of us learn to master the ability to identify that source and start maintaining it. And for the ones of us that do, the recognition of contentment often starts later in life, unless we deliberately set out to discover and nurture it early on.

Now, being content with your current situation doesn't necessarily mean that you don't ever change it. But you need a balance point first, a position from which you can oversee your strengths, weaknesses, opportunities, and threats, before you can decide upon a useful direction, followed by an appropriate strategy. In business, they call this point, where you make an evaluation to choose a future direction, a SWOT analysis, which is an acronym for Strengths, Weaknesses, Opportunities, and Threats. And you can only make this analysis if you know where you currently stand. The misperception of many of us is that SWOT analyses only pertain to work-related matters: to organizations. But, like organizations, human beings also have a mission, a vision, and—sometimes unconscious—a strategy. Besides, it's not hard to understand management gurus when they explain that we should start perceiving ourselves as organizations, and our employers as clients.

Contentment is, thus, the point where we can oversee our position, feel good about it, and then determine whether we prefer to leave it this way, or gradually want to work toward a different goal. Gradually, because we know that most overnight decisions turn into catastrophes.

It's also the level of contentment within us that will enable us to change focus when something seems unachievable, yet keep faith in ourselves, and—consequentially—our dignity.

You can ask any leader who has made a deep impression in multiple settings, what kept them sane in the most difficult moments of their career. Nine times out of ten you will find something in their list of capacities and traits that could be translated as contentment or serenity. It has a lot to do with the ability to remain serene under the most critical circumstances, because this is what enables people to see opportunities where others see threats and to dismantle the disguise in which the most lucrative chances sometimes present themselves. It may sound contradictive, but being at peace with your current position will allow you to reach greater heights than you ever considered possible, while restless fighting against your situation will only lead to painful encounters with people who perceive you as a threat and a power-hawk.

The serenity prayer teaches us to accept things we cannot change, change things we can, and know the difference. And that's exactly what it's all about. Contentment is a crucial state of being under all circumstances, whether life is flowing like a calm river, or whether it runs wild like a waterfall.

One last note: contentment cannot be kept at its highest level all the time. There will be moments that it seems as if it simply isn't there. For instance, when your normal routine is disturbed by temporary restrictions, unforeseen setbacks, or other circumstances that you cannot change. The COVID-19 global pandemic is an excellent example of a disturbed routine—for more people in the world at the same time than usually happens.

All you can do in such moments is to sit back and reduce your sense of resentment or panic by practicing inner contentment or serenity. If the setback is just short-lived, you can put yourself on autopilot, do the most necessary things on your schedule, and wait until the disruption fades. Oftentimes it leaves as sudden as it came. But there are instances when the disruption lasts longer, such as the one with the Novel Coronavirus (better known as COVID-19), which changed our status quo for much longer than we ever thought to be possible. In such instances, you should determine when it's time to start looking for a solution and a possible change in your life circumstances in order to reach a new point of contentment.

The serenity source, being the deep breath you take, the moments of thoughts you lapse into, and the evaluation you consequentially make, will lead you toward the new level of contentment in which you will feel satisfied. Just remember,

> The outward freedom that we shall attain will only be in exact to the inward freedom to which we may have grown at a given moment. And this is a correct view of freedom, our chief energy must be concentrated on achieving reform from within.
>
> *Mohandas K. Gandhi, as cited in Dalton (2012, p. 7)*

Reference

Dalton, D. (2012). *Mahatma Gandhi: Nonviolent Power in Action*. Columbia University Press, New York, NY.

6

SUPPORTING/NOT HARMING

In the Hindu, Buddhist, and Jain tradition, there is a term, "ahimsa," which entails nonviolence toward all living things. One of the best-known statements from the Dalai Lama is also related to this concept. He advises to help wherever we can, and if we cannot help, we should at least refrain from harming. The quality of being supportive and connected with others, especially in today's hectic workplaces, is not easy to find. Supervisors and managers are so absorbed with performance rules that they often forget, in spite of their good intentions, to be supportive and try to find ways to protect their employees from being harmed.

Yet, being supportive can have a positive long-term effect that we should not underestimate. Here's a story to illustrate:

> Mr. Dawson was the most powerful man at QRS, a [fictitious] company specialized in the development of quality research systems. He had been the president of the company for over 10 years. However, only a few of the top managers at QRS had ever seen him. The program developers, sales-people in the stores, and even the office managers had no clue what Mr. Dawson looked like. Some of them even believed the rumor that Mr. Dawson did not really exist. But no one really dared talking about it, because there were also whispers that some employees, who had joked about Mr. Dawson's vague state of being, had been fired in spite of their good performance.
>
> At the end of every year, there was a seasonal gift packet for every employee in the conference room. This packet was granted on top of the bonuses. However, the end-of-year celebrations, including the speeches and other annual ceremonies were executed by the respective managers.
>
> Mr. Dawson was powerful, indeed, even though he was not a very caring person, and did not seem to worry about the well-being of his

employees. Several people in the company even claimed that he was a billionaire. And, although never seen, he seemed to have his ears everywhere in the organization, which inhibited employees to speak up freely about their ideas regarding this invisible man, who seems to lead by fear.

Samuel was one of the managers at QRS. He had worked at the company for 10 years, and never missed a day at work. At least, not without a very good reason, like that one time when his mother passed away unexpectedly.

Everyone in the company liked Samuel because he was open, caring, and empathetic. He could always be found on the work floor, where he had a kind word ready for everybody he met: not only his employees but also the ones that were not directly linked to his department as well. Samuel was in fact more of a mentor figure. People all through the organization would call him to ask his advice on issues that oftentimes were very personal.

Samuel's department was the one at QRS where everyone wanted to work. There was a relaxed atmosphere in the office, and his staff seemed to have developed a wonderful subculture. There were trust and openness, and the Monday morning meetings were always held in a very pleasant ambiance. Sometimes even outside in the open air! Every week someone took care of the doughnuts that were literally inhaled during the sessions. There was a lot of humor, and the entire spirit was one of creativity encouragement. Ideas were never discarded without team contemplation, and his employees knew that if they brought something up, Samuel would go to the limit to get their point across. Now, he didn't always succeed in getting all wishes granted, but no one held that against him, because they knew he tried.

Samuel was influential, but even more: he was supportive and tried to refrain from harming anyone. His advice was important to many people throughout QRS, not only professionally but also in private areas as well.

At some point, Samuel decided to start his own company in research systems and other computer software services. He aimed to start small and gave his notice according to the company rules. No one liked to see this wonderful man go. More strikingly, many of the very best employees at QRS started applying for jobs at Samuel's new company.

Within two years the company had expanded into a successful middle-sized organization, where suppliers, customers, and employees were all happy and contented. The company could have been much larger, for there was enough interest from all sides, not in the least customers. But Samuel wanted to keep the connective spirit intact, and he realized that this would be harder if the company grew too fast. His conviction was that the organization's performance should not necessarily rest on moneymaking, but on excellent performance from a happy workforce. The company's core purpose was, appropriately, "To accommodate America's knowledge workforce by providing the highest quality in products and service through teamwork, creativity, and trust."

And QRS? That organization ultimately went out of business. After Samuel left, several other managers decided to either start their own businesses as well or find a job in a work environment where it was much more fun. To all workers, QRS had served its purpose as a stepping stone in their career, but the lack of personal approach and the coercive atmosphere ultimately drove the best workers away.

The powerful but uncaring Mr. Dawson remained wealthy for the rest of his vague days, although his power could be questioned on the long run, and the supportive, well-appreciated Samuel is still going strong in the market of computer research software.

PART III

What's the Foundational Problem?

7

LACK OF UNDERSTANDING

Lack of understanding actually has a deeper foundation: it is either ingrained in unwillingness to take the time to understand, or it rests on deep-rooted biases, which stand in the way of the willpower to learn more about the source of the misunderstanding.

When we lack interest or are too deeply engaged in another mindset or practice, we find it hard to take the time to collaborate with those we don't understand. It is one of the common pitfalls for leaders, especially those who perform in a high-stress environment. It is so much easier to gravitate toward those that walk, talk, and behave like you, as a leader, than to learn the reasons behind the behaviors and decisions of those that are "different."

This, then, is the foundation for in-groups and out-groups in workplaces. What are those? An in-group is the team of people a leader likes to surround him or herself with because they understand one another. Most of the time, the members of this group have similar backgrounds and interests as the leader, which makes them more trustworthy in the perspective of the leader.

And then there is the out-group: those folks are the "others," whom the leader feels little affinity with, either because they represent a different culture, think and behave differently, or hold perspectives the leader doesn't agree with. You may have heard the term "othering," which is often experienced by minority groups in work and other social settings. It takes a lot of inner strength to continue generating inspiration in a workplace where the leadership team considers and treats you as an "other." It is particularly demoralizing when you see how colleagues get so much more done with far less effort than you.

It is therefore critical, as current and future leaders, to reflect on this notion. If you don't like to be in the position of being an "other," work toward inclusion. Take the time to listen to others, and give them similar opportunities compared to those you feel an initial attraction to. The effect will be enhanced understanding, which will lead to increased mutual appreciation, a greater sense of ownership, more productivity from more angles, and a tremendous surge in motivation.

8

TAKER MINDSET

This section is an attempt to illustrate the hypocrisy we so often encounter in modern thinking. Remember that we're trying to find out in this section what the foundational problem is in society and leadership. It's, in one short term, the "taker mindset," which we have become accustomed to adopt as the most proper one. Foundational to understanding the taker mindset is Daniel Quinn's inspirational book "Ishmael" and the movie "Instinct," based on Quinn's book.

Ishmael presents the story of a gorilla that taught a man to look at "modern civilization" from an outsider's point of view. It quickly becomes apparent that the dominating theme in society is control: controlling one's behavior, position, status, and property. Laws increasingly show that there is something amiss with our collective perception of freedom.

One of the ways modern society controls the fate of its members is through the application of the death penalty. In 2020, 17 prisoners were executed in the United States. Five states and the Federal Government carried out executions. On the other hand, the US society has a problem with the individual desire to end one's life, even if one suffers immensely and death is inevitable. Euthanasia is still taboo in several of the United States, even for the terminally ill. This is particularly peculiar when we consider how often the United States is referred to as a "free country."

The movie Instinct, which is based on the book Ishmael, also emphasizes the issue of control. Humans consider themselves the ultimate powerhouse of the world: thereby exterminating everything that does not bow or bend.

For more clarity, let's briefly review Daniel Quinn's "Ishmael." Ishmael, a gorilla, challenges his human pupil to deeply examine himself and his kind, and to figure out what "mother culture" has taught society. Using the expression "Take it or leave it" as a basis, Ishmael divides mankind into two categories:

Takers and Leavers. The Takers are those who have been indoctrinated by their churches and prophets to believe that the world belongs to man (Quinn, 1992), that man is the center of the universe, and that everything should serve man. The Takers were also taught that there is only one right way of living (Quinn, 1992), and were thereby forced to adapt to lifestyles that often did not even fit their geographical and physical circumstances.

Taker culture has become a culture of expansion, one of neglecting the laws of nature, one of "caring for the poor," an act that, even though fundamentally noble, has erupted into the current population explosion due to the erroneous way in which it is performed. According to Quinn, Taker culture has also become one of destroying everything that crosses its path. It has evolved into a culture to save, to store, and especially to not rely on the gods but solely on oneself, because Takers want to take matters into their own hands: they want to be in control. The Taker culture is what we now know as modern civilization.

The Leavers, according to Ishmael, are the peoples that have always been hunted down by the Takers. They live by the rule: man belongs to the world. Their culture develops as a result of the circumstances under which they are living. Leavers realize that there is no one right way to live (Quinn, 1992).

Ishmael explains that there are three hard lessons the Taker society must learn.

1. The earth is NOT the center of the universe.
2. Man evolved, like all other creatures, from the common slime of the earth.
3. The gods did not exempt man from the law that governs the lives of all other creatures. Species that do not live in compliance with the law become extinct.

Takers, therefore, have to realize that their culture does not "fly," but is heading for a fatal crash, unless they restart obeying the rules of the game. Lesson 3 will be the hardest to accept by the Takers (aka modern society). It will require an awakening and a renewed respect for natural laws, thereby putting mother culture— the foundation of the Takers' perception of uniqueness and superiority—to sleep forever. Ishmael is analyzing how things came to be the way they are by explaining that the Taker and Leaver cultures were initially the same. However, at a certain point in time, somewhere in the fertile land between the Euphrates and the Tigris, Adam (Semite for "man"), ate from the forbidden tree of "knowledge of good and evil," and was tempted by Eve (Semite for "life"). From then on man thought he was God. He concluded that he was the ruler of the world, having the power to decide who should live and who should die. The story of Adam should not be seen as the start of mankind, but as the start of Taker culture . . . or agricultural revolution (Quinn, 1992).

Referring to the Biblical book "Genesis," Ishmael asserts that this should be interpreted as a parable, in which Cain is the symbol of man in Taker culture, and Abel is the symbol of man in Leaver culture. Abel, explains Ishmael, is still very much alive, though hunted down wherever Cain can find him. Abel is nowadays represented by the hunter–gatherers, which are called "primitive" by the Takers, because they don't save and store for tomorrow, but they remained unsuspecting and naive enough through time to continue living in the hands of the gods. Leavers still live with the trust that the world will regularly provide food. And if that does not happen they die, because dying is no shame to them. They are therefore never confronted with the problem of overpopulation, yet they survive! Cain, on the other hand, is represented by the agrarian culture of storing, killing off everything that disrupts his plans (Quinn, 1992, p. 132), and hence, bringing the whole system out of balance. Cain is "us."

Instinct

Every now and then an attempt is made to alert modern society about the destructive course it has taken. Like Ishmael, the movie Instinct can be seen as a wake-up call that can be either ignored or noticed.

Instinct, based on Daniel Quinn's above-discussed novel Ishmael, shows the story of a brilliant primatologist, Dr. Ethan Powell, who finds his truth in the jungles of Rwanda. The reviewing website on this movie exclaims that Powell's truth was derived from years of studying mountain gorillas—to the point where he was living among them in the wild, and accepted as one of their own (Instinct, 1999). Powell adapts to the freeway of living that these gorillas teach him. His most eye-opening experience is the newly gained perception that the world he was raised in is a "Taker world," where the only thing that matters is power and control. When a search-troop attacks the gorillas, Powell turns against humanity and kills many of the attackers before he is captured. Held captive in a prison for the criminally insane, Powell, who has not spoken in years, is visited for treatment by psychiatrist Theo Caulder. The young Dr. Caulder's ambition drives him to risk everything and put his career on the line to understand the actions of this headline-gripping madman.

The movie shows the touching metamorphoses in the ambitious psychiatrist, while he succeeds in persuading Powell to talk to him. Powell starts to share his memories of Rwanda and teaches Caulder about the "Takers" and "Leavers" and a kind of revisionist history of mankind, how we went wrong and how we got to the place we are. As Caulder begins the task of trying to understand Powell, he becomes overwhelmed by his story and the tables turn so that instead of psychiatrist and prisoner, it becomes student and teacher.

The stunning realization that the freedom in our society decreases as the order increases; will most likely become apparent to everyone who reads the book "Ishmael," or views the movie "Instinct." These two sources emphasize the necessity to regain our awareness on the importance of natural laws and provide the reader/viewer insight in the fact that the rules and regulations of our society have become wedged to a ridiculous point. The Taker culture, created by religious beliefs that "man is the ruler of the world," has led to a gruesome point where mankind behaves as if there is no God. The most interesting part of it all is that we defend our acts by teaching our fellow humans that this is what God wants!

Our Taker culture is in trouble, and perhaps that's not a bad thing given its many flaws. Yet, human society has a chance to be saved if we can reach the point of maturity in our thinking; if we realize that many of our boundaries are inherited by beliefs that date back to a time in which our knowledge about our place in the universe was far more limited—and thus more arrogant—than it is or should be today.

References

Execution List 2020. Retrieved from https://deathpenaltyinfo.org/executions/2020.
Instinct. (1999). Retrieved from www.imdb.com/title/tt0128278/.
Quinn, D. (1992). *Ishmael*. Bantam Books, Incorporated, New York, NY.

9

HURT AND AVERSION

Humans are creatures of habit. We cherish some habits and have a hard time releasing others. This is also the case with embracing new colleagues and releasing old ones at work. While adapting to incoming parties may require some time, we rather welcome new friends or colleagues than release old ones. Similarly, we dread changes in our work schedule, location, or content. It is especially the process of shifting from an old status quo to a new one that we struggle with and feel hurt about.

Bridges (2009) explains this as the difference between change and transition: change is the completion of a transition. It is therefore the transition that we should be sensitive about, because that's when the change is created. It's like picking up a chess pawn: once the pawn is replaced, the change has happened, and the moving-on process can start. Bridges recommends allowing those left behind to mourn the changed situation after a transition, which is sound advice. Once people have mourned a transition, they may appreciate, even celebrate, a new beginning.

A habit that helps even more than struggling with and mourning transitions is what I call, "healthy detachment," which derives from Buddhist psychology. It reminds us that all suffering comes from two states of mind: attachment and aversion. These two mindsets cause us to be in an almost continuous state of mental commotion, because there are always things (processes, places, and, yes, people) we're attached to, and others we resent. And even though it's not easy to develop the habit of healthy detachment, it's a great one to maintain once acquired.

Think about it this way: workplaces are miniature replicas of life—things come and go continuously, and nothing remains the same forever. The law of impermanence is as present in the workplace as anywhere else. Security is a great term, but it's a surreal construct, erected in our minds to feel at ease, because many of us dislike the lack of security that is our life. Yet, regardless of the height of our bank account or our prominence, we have no guarantee that we'll see our next moment.

Arising and Passing

One of the most important lessons I internalized in management and life practices is arising and passing. Everything arises and passes, and our breath constantly reminds us of this reality. We inhale, which manifests arising, and we exhale, which embodies passing. It's a process we continuously repeat, but rarely pay attention to, unless we land in a situation where our breathing is obstructed.

An effective way of gaining breathing awareness is through Vipassana meditation. S. N. Goenka, a businessman turned meditation teacher, initiated the Vipassana movement from Burma to India and subsequently to the rest of the world. Goenka, who passed away in 2013, explained that Vipassana meditation can help us gain mastery over the mind with morality at its foundation, so we can develop experiential wisdom to eliminate the emotional destructions of attachment and aversion (Goenka, 2001). Once we realize that we are disrupting our inner peace through excessive attachment and aversion, we may become more wakeful and understand the waves that make up for our life.

The awareness of arising and passing, thus the need for letting go, can also be achieved through other ways. Regularly reflecting on our breathing and how it resembles everything around us can help us internalize that it's no use to get overly attached or averse to anything, regardless how much we like, dread, appreciate, or abhor it. It will, ultimately, be gone, just like everything else, including ourselves.

A non-meditative but equally effective way of reminding ourselves about arising and passing is an observation of the sea waves: some small and calm, others majestic and intimidating. Yet, they all pass after arising, for others to continue the cycle. Similarly, we can reflect on the peaks and valleys of our life: graduation, marriage, childbirth, pet adoption, landing our job, but also losing a loved one, moving away from our birthplace, losing a job, getting a divorce: those were all moments that arose, left their mark, and then passed, for others to emerge.

This is not a call to abandon every type of attachment, because there is something to be said about desires and attaching ourselves to progress in life. If we had no desires to obtain anything and no aversions to escape anything, no one would attempt to rise above any situation, regardless of how bad! People get ahead when they desire to raise their living standards, which is commendable. Without craving for improvement and aversion about the status quo, creativity and strive for excellence would not exist. People need a reason, a purpose, to perform. Nothing wrong with that. However, there should also be an elevated awareness about these goals: a realization that whatever we achieve will not always be there, so we should be flexible to learn from every encounter and move on (Marques, 2008).

Letting Go as a Remedy to Aversion and Hurt

Not everyone understands or appreciates the Buddhist psychology of leading and maintaining oneself, especially in work environments. Not being attached in a social setting may seem antisocial, aloof, or even self-obstructive, and may get colleagues on guard, especially in cultures where people like socializing. Yet, that is a misconstrued notion.

Healthy detachment does not make people insensitive. It just helps them see matters in a larger perspective: everything is in constant flux, and when people are released from a certain environment it simply means that they have to move into a different one. Oftentimes, this may even be one that fits their interests and passions better than the current one. I recall several colleagues who were released from their job, and ultimately discovered their path toward a completely different career that they might have desired, but would never have explored, had they stayed in their previous job. I have seen colleagues using their layoff to embark upon further education, and later land jobs that did not only pay much better but also provided them more satisfaction (Marques, 2020).

Because the insight of letting go is so personal, yet so valuable to everyone, organizations could consider forming storytelling gatherings, open to all employees with a need for personal and professional encouragement. At those gatherings, which should be kept informal and optional, some employees could take the lead in sharing positive stories of the good that came after a seemingly disastrous occurrence. While circumstances may differ from one shared experience to another, the message will soon be clear that there is sunshine after rain, and that togetherness helps when courage and understanding are needed. As a point of caution: these sessions should be monitored by strong, positive-minded colleagues, in order to prevent disintegration into demoralizing complaint sessions.

Being aware that everything arises and passes can help us become less attached to our titles and positions, and help us move on. If we are amongst those left behind, we may understand that our colleagues are ready for the next stage in their lives, and send them positive vibes rather than mourning their departure (Marques, 2020).

Our inability to see in the future makes us vulnerable to the occurrences of today. While it may be tough to develop and maintain healthy detachment, it could be the most balanced way of going through life and reducing the sense of aversion and hurt that so often overwhelms us. It definitely helps with understanding and even appreciating the process of letting go when others are mourning, oftentimes troubled by grudges, fear, and demoralization. Healthy detachment is not aimed to lead to aloofness but rather to nurture understanding that everything will turn out right in the larger scheme of things, and that arising and passing are natural progressions of life.

References

Bridges, W. (2009). *Managing Transitions: Making the Most of Change.* Perseus Press, New York, NY.

Goenka, S. N. (2001). *Was the Buddha a Pessimist?* Vipassana Research Institute, Dhammagiri, Igatpuri.

Marques, J. (2008). The golden midway: Arising and passing on the road to personal and professional excellence. *Interbeing, 2*(2), pp. 5–10.

Marques, J. (2020). Letting go: The art of arts. *Development and Learning in Organizations.* Vol. ahead-of-print No. ahead-of-print. https://doi.org/10.1108/DLO-09-2019-0221.

PART IV
How Can I Solve It?

10

REFLECTING

Inwardly and Outwardly

As the demands and the pace of life increase all around us, we cannot escape the desire at times to return to a life in which we can value the simple things again. In fact, that's not impossible: we can keep ourselves afloat and even thriving in today's VUCA (volatile, uncertain, complex, and ambiguous) world while we engage in regular reflections to keep ourselves grounded. In this section, we will consider how we can perform in our daily lives, while also dwelling on the simple gifts we all received in our lives, many of which we tend to take for granted, thus overlook.

The Paradox of Our Times

We are living in intriguing times. Never before has humanity had this degree of sophistication in communicating with such advanced devices on such an expansive scale. At the same time, we have grown closer than ever before to the understanding that we have to rethink many of the paths we threaded so far. Whether we accept the theories about global warming or not, we cannot deny that there is little reason for pride when we think of the many manifestations of corporate deception led by the seemingly insatiable greed of small groups of people. The question remains how we can balance these two factors, which basically boil down to an interesting paradox: we face more distraction, while we realize the need for greater focus.

The most critical thing about regaining focus is that it works differently for each of us. There is no specific lecture or seminar we can take to start refocusing on what really matters. Yet, one thing may work for many of us: dwelling just a little bit longer on all those small gifts we have by the very virtue of being alive.

These are gifts we easily overlook, because they are there, and no one questions or discusses them on a daily basis.

Here are three of the gifts we regularly overlook.

1.   The gift of you.

A lady once had a precious necklace around her neck. But, forgetful as we can all be sometimes, she forgot that she had it on and thought that her necklace was lost. She looked for it everywhere but could not find it. She called friends and family members to ask if they knew the whereabouts of her precious necklace, but none of them had any idea where it could be. At last one of her friends suggested for her to feel around her neck to find out if, perhaps, she was wearing it? She felt around her neck and, indeed, found that the necklace had been there all along. In the days after her frantic search, the lady's friends and family members called her to ask if she found her necklace. She admitted to finding it, because to her it was as if she had lost it, even though it had been with her all the time.

Just as it is with the precious piece of jewelry of the lady, so is it too with ourselves. We often forget our most important gift, our self—which is always with us—and seek everything we need outside. We ask friends and family members, mentors, colleagues, supervisors, gurus, and others to advise us about issues to which we could actually find the best answers by turning to the jewel inside.

Many people are skeptical about this notion of an inner guru. That is because they have been programmed so well and so long to rely on everything and everybody else for counsel, that they no longer believe they harbor the capacity to develop insights. Some of them visit the inner fountain at times and then forget about it again, as they get caught in the demanding quests of life. Others may initially turn inward and find answers but then get influenced by an externally focused environment, upon which they promptly lose touch with their core.

Nevertheless, all the awareness you need in life resides inside of you. A good way to reconnect with this inner wealth is through meditation. Meditation is not a religious process, but more a psychological one. And just as well as we have been psychologically conditioned to think that insight and awareness are external treasures to be chased continuously, we can psychologically recondition ourselves to understand that they reside inside.

Sir Ken Robinson, one of the most brilliant critics of our education system, gives a funny but telling example of a little girl who is drawing something. When her teacher asks her what she's drawing she says, "I'm drawing God." The teacher says, "But no one knows what God looks like!" Little girl: "They will in a minute."

There was a time you were like that little girl, with a similar connection to your inner awareness and imagination. You can restore that connection and rediscover the path to your inner fountain and its abundance. Try it. It may be an enjoyable journey!

2.   The gift of breathing

You may have heard people say that we only value something when we have lost it. That is very true. But there is one thing that's so critical, that we no longer exist once we lost it: our breath.

Day after day, we are so busy undertaking all kinds of "important" actions, that we take the things that really matter for granted. Breathing is one of those things. How often do we simply take a moment to focus on our breathing? And yet, it is the one thing that distinguishes us from death. But because we have been blessed with this gift from birth, we don't think about it too often. We rarely value it, until there is a moment when we get in trouble and cannot breathe. That moment can be a minuscule one. Just a few seconds. When the air is cut off, we suddenly realize that all those appointments, living standards, desires, special someone's, positions, and possessions don't really matter. When our breath gets cut off, we are ready to sacrifice all those "important" things to get it back.

There is a touching story of a man who suffered from asthma. He just met a pretty young lady, and they were getting along very well. Yet, about a week after they met, while making plans to go to the movies, he got a terrible asthma attack. It was so severe that his friend realized she had to do something drastic. She stopped a passing car and explained the problem. As they raced to the hospital, the young man's breath stopped completely. However, his girlfriend was not planning to let him slip away, and she performed cardiopulmonary resuscitation (CPR) onto him over and over again until they reached their destination, where he was rushed inside and placed on a ventilator. By giving him her breath, he stayed alive. They are now happily married and have a family. It would not have been possible without sharing her breath in those critical moments.

Breathing is possible through the air around us, and we all know that we would not survive if that was gone. The earth, our common home, harbors the right amount of oxygen and the perfect temperature to provide us with the conditions to stay alive. But that, too, is something we don't consider often enough. Instead, we mainly focus on things that disrupt our peace of mind, such as trying to own a more advanced car than our neighbor, or wear a more expensive dress than our friend, or acquire a higher position than our colleague. We want to impress, and we are filled with the ambition to do so. That's not necessarily a bad thing, as long as it does not become such an obsession that it entirely disrupts our joy in life. It is critical to regularly keep the bigger picture in mind, and the funny thing is, that the bigger picture is captured in the modest things. But without the basic conditions, which we all share and need, there would be none of our daily strife.

So, here's to the gift of breathing.

3. The gift of today

The fact that you are reading this now indicates that you received the gift of being alive, the gift of reading, the gift of understanding, the gift of the medium through which you read this, and the gift of time to do so. Along with all these gifts come others, such as the gift of breathing in order to be alive, and the gift of thinking in order to understand.

While you may or may not take all these gifts for granted: there is one you most surely forget to appreciate as a gift now and then: the gift of today. In spite of the fact that we call today the present, we often take it for granted because we get caught in so many other things: hectic schedules, concerns about our health, our financial situation, work-related problems, family or other issues, you name it. But today is here: it came and is slowly progressing. It will last exactly 24 hours, which equals 1,440 minutes, or 86,400 seconds. Today resembles our life in that regard: it is limited and dying from the moment it is born. Here are three important thoughts to consider about today:

1. Once today is gone, it never comes back, so everything you do now will be history from tomorrow on. If you behave rash and do something you regret later, you may try to correct it—and even succeed—but you will never be able to undo it. This also means that today is an important foundation for the rest of your life, because you are making choices and decisions that will affect your future.
2. You have a limited number of days available in your life, and no one knows how many you have left. Anything that is available in a limited supply is considered a scarce good in economic terms. With everything becoming increasingly edgy, and the pace of life picking up continuously, this scarce day cannot be wasted. Of course, it depends on you to determine what "wasting" your day looks like, but I'm sure you know.
3. Today is a great beginning, because it's the first day of the rest of your life. No matter what you did in the past: today offers you a chance to start something wonderful. If there is a dream you wanted to realize, today is a good day to seriously start working on it. If you wanted to change a bad habit or correct something wrong, today is a great day to do that. There is nothing that cannot happen today, so why not make it happen?

There is an infinite supply of gifts to our disposal, which we enjoy, yet overlook as being gifts, until we are in danger of losing them. There is no need to let it get so far. We can start enjoying a happier life from here on if we stop now and then, and reflect on some of our invaluable gifts, which make us the special beings we are today.

11

QUESTIONING MY ACTIONS

Contemplating on Security and Progress

MIND, BODY, AND . . . ?

Moving from present to future
And oftentimes also to the past
Able to imagine alternatives
To situations that didn't last
Rarely dwelling too long anywhere
Shifting, now slow, then fast
An avid traveler at its core
Here calm, but there with a blast

Like a disloyal partner it moves
Away from the body and back
In directions hard to predict
Ever flowing, alert—rarely slack
Conjuring mesmerizing thoughts
Colorful, bright, or pitch-black
Harder to pin down as you try
And not easy to keep on track

Captured in my head but not caught
The fountain of many a thought
Not even slowing down during sleep
Crossing continents in a swift leap

> And if someday it stays away
> This body might be led astray
> And then will come the day I die
> But then I wonder: who am I?
>
> ~ Joan Marques

There are many terms we use every day that have distinctive meaning to us. Success, wealth, love, care, and happiness are some good examples. We use these terms frequently, and we rarely reflect on whether others have the same interpretation of them as we do. Over the years, I have found that security and progress are also among the terms that depend heavily on personal interpretation. We talk about security in the context of our jobs, homes, and/or families. In reality, however, does security mean the same thing to everyone who uses the term in association with these factors? Similarly, we use the word "progress" to indicate some kind of movement ahead, but does one person's determination of progress always align with others' perceptions? As leaders of our lives, and in our dealings with others, we should be very reflective of that. This section presents a brief scenario and discussion related to both of these terms.

The Illusion of Security

A number of years ago a colleague suggested that I should accept a full-time position. A position recently had opened, and he felt that I should apply—not only because I had the right credentials but also because he felt that I would "be more secure" as I would receive primary and secondary benefits if I became a full-time employee. I couldn't help but smile because the expression "being secure" always has that effect on me. Why do we always want to be secure? Admittedly, seeking security is an ingrained human tendency. On the other hand, how many of us have learned that security is a farce? If even our next breath isn't secure, how could any process, position, or relationship be? We often live with the idea that our jobs provide security. In real life, however, how secure are our jobs? Even if our supervisors promise solemnly that they will not release us because we're such valuable workers, who guarantees that the promise will remain unchanged? They may move somewhere else tomorrow, change their minds, or the company may merge with another firm causing everyone to be dismissed. The list of potential circumstances that might affect the supervisors' commitment is almost endless. At the same time, we may choose to do something else with our lives and leave our jobs proactively.

In the 2008 economic downturn, and again during the 2020 COVID-19 pandemic, many experienced the deception of economic security. In a concise, but strong piece, P. O'Sullivan (2012) reminds us that our world is not a risk-free place.

Even "risk-free bonds" were so risky in the 2008 financial crisis that banks turned to bailouts to avoid collapse. He then reveals the interesting other side of the coin; when people are released from a false sense of security, they become more careful and get into less trouble. The example he provides is Drachten, a small town in the Netherlands, where all traffic lights and road signs were removed, which promptly led to a zero rate of fatal accidents, due to the heightened caution of drivers and pedestrians alike. In private matters, security is also a slippery subject. People get married and promise to love and cherish one another till death parts them. Then, within five years, many go their separate ways. Although some of the couples who experienced a change of heart may decide to stay together for a variety of reasons, they remain bitter for the rest of their lives. Of course, there are the precious few who truly remain happy together for an extended amount of time, which is beautiful.

The point remains that when we stand at the commencement of a personal or private situation, it always seems so promising, and we think that it will be a "sure, lasting shot." This happens through a combination of two factors—being captured at the moment and carrying a deeply embedded longing for security. Nevertheless, humans are interesting creatures who don't differ that much from animals. Fundamentally, we are just as capricious as other living organisms, which leads to us discovering that as time goes by, our desires and interests subside or disappear in one area and emerge or increase in another.

In the meantime, however, we may have secured ourselves in relationships or contracts. So we find ourselves going through tremendous pains to exit those situations without experiencing too much peril. In these situations, others may criticize us as being unreliable. This internal tension between a yearning for security on one hand and a natural mental/emotional flux on the other can be very confusing and difficult to deal with in many circumstances. The internal ambivalence can be muddled further by an increased pace of change around us. In an eye-opening article, Dragan Staniševski (2011) examines the general sense of "ontological security" which we embrace naturally. Ontological relates to being, becoming, or existing. Staniševski's article explains that we may be aware that illness, unemployment, social unrest, or other commotions can strike at any time, but we continue to yearn for a sense of security because it helps us function. After all, to perform we need a certain level of trust in the continuation of previously experienced events. We are confronted with many anxieties that begin in childhood and continue throughout our lives, but we learn to detect recurring patterns that provide a sense of stability. As we grow, our expanding social contacts enhance our understanding of societal do's and don'ts. These help us build a defensive barrier as well as a national self in which we learn to identify with our culture, nation, the many groups to which we belong, and everything they represent. Staniševski warns, however, that we live in an increasingly interconnected world where instability seems to be the new normal. Although it might be difficult, if not impossible, to release our longing for security entirely, we may find that embracing a more multidimensional self-perception works better than maintaining the traditional individual notion of who we are. This is particularly important as we experience increased exposure to members from other societies and deal with almost continuously accelerating, heightening change and instability.

The Capricious Notion of Progress

A while ago, an old friend called from the Netherlands. He owns a small factory there and seems satisfied with his life. Although he calls regularly to make small talk, he had a special reason for contacting me this time. He had been speaking with a mutual friend, and together they concluded that I should visit them to explore options to immigrate. Both friends felt that I could do fabulous things and experience tremendous growth in the Netherlands. Just when this proposal started to sound really good to my sense of adventure, my friend made a comment that stirred me from my daze of fascination. He stated that after more than a decade of running stationary, it was time for me to get into some "real action" again. I was baffled! Here was a challenging journey of earning advanced degrees, publishing books, writing more than 400 articles, giving lectures and presentations, organizing conferences and workshops, and cofounding nonprofit organizations and scholarly journals thrown on the heap of "stationary"—no progress! So I asked what he meant by the phrase "running stationary," and he summarized his opinion by restating the word "stationary." I pondered his comment and realized that my two friends had a different perspective—their focus probably was based on financial growth rather than intellectual or spiritual development. Indeed, in the first 20 years of my working life, I had focused on finances by gathering as many assets as possible, intending to retire early at 40 and enjoy life. After 19 of those 20 years, however, I realized that merely gathering material wins was no longer a thrill, so I set out for a much more rewarding life—one with far less extrinsic incentives but with tremendously more intrinsic satisfaction. The trade-offs made sense to me—no expensive cars but lots of elated moments, no impressive mansion but a tremendous sense of serenity, no glamorous reputation that resulted in a massive bank account but numerous spirit-lifting projects that helped people from all over the world grow, less financial luxury but more peace of mind, less selfishness but more connectivity, and fewer spotlights but more enlightenment.

It is through that realization that I became abundantly aware that our personal perception of progress drives what motivates us. Progress is not necessarily manifested in the level of external change that becomes visible; it also may involve major spiritual evolution. In a 2002 article about futures studies, Marcus Bussey highlighted the difference between change and progress, explaining that change mainly involves material developments, while progress is of a spiritual nature, intertwined in our own conscious evolution. In that same year, four researchers led by Doug Newburg (Newburg et al., 2002) developed a model in which they described how resonance can make us aware of the type of progress that will be meaningful to us. In this case, resonance occurs when there is a seamless fit between the internal self and the external environment. The process of achieving resonance requires us to search ourselves and understand how we would like to feel about ourselves. We ask the critical question, "What is preventing us from becoming resonant?" Once we have formulated our analysis of these critical concerns, we can work toward eliminating the barriers and achieve our desired feelings, which the authors refer to as "the dream." They clarify that freedom and responsibility are important prerequisites to having this dream because these two factors drive the process of resonance. When I considered these authors' descriptions of the components of progress—particularly the spiritual factor—it became clear how the misunderstanding between my friends' perceptions and my own had occurred. Although my friends still perceived that material development equated with progress, I had evolved toward a new focus—identifying and realizing my dream through resonance.

As the two scenarios in this chapter demonstrate, security and progress have very individual, personalized meanings. It is important to reflect on that, and be sensitive about such multi-interpretable, yet critical concepts. Our desire to establish security may have a negative effect on our sense of happiness. In our quest for security, we create social structures that may curtail our natural passion, placing us in unhappy positions where others are dictating what will be good for us (or not good for us). This may result in an increasing number of society's members stepping out of line. In times when there were fewer changes and those changes were more local (less international), we created a sense of overall durability, which is now obsolete.

Today, more than ever, nothing is secure—our jobs, positions, statuses, relationships, or even our lives. Everything may be different tomorrow. So security is a paradox; although many of us consider it to be important and continually pursue it, in reality it is unattainable. If we perceive life as being naturally in a state of flux, we will be better prepared, avoiding disappointment. We can be more relaxed in our approach toward everything. We can view each relationship as a gift to cherish as long as it lasts, understanding that we may have to let go at some point in the future because nothing is permanently secure.

In regard to progress, it should be clarified that although it is not necessary to avoid material advancement totally, we need to remain vigilant about overemphasizing this as a priority, which may result in the loss of far more important essentials, such as peace of mind and personal gratification. Treading a more balanced path is the key to real progress in life. The conversations with my colleague and my overseas friend taught me to think differently. Opinions associated with terms such as security and progress vary greatly, depending on individual perspectives and experiences. Others may view the security and progress associated with our lives much differently than we do. In the end, however, these different perspectives should not be a problem because security and progress are assessed by our personal definitions—the decisions we have made as individuals regarding their application to our lives.

References

Bussey, M. (2002). From change to progress: Critical spirituality and the futures of futures studies. *Futures*, *34*(3–4), pp. 303–315.

Newburg, D. S., Kimiecik, J. C., Durand-Bush, N., & Doell, K. (2002). The role of resonance in performance excellence and life engagement. *Journal of Applied Sport Psychology*, *14*(4), pp. 249–267.

O'Sullivan, P. (July 8, 2012). False sense of security. *The Sunday Times* [serial online], p. 2.

Staniševski, D. (2011). Fear thy neighbor: Ontological security and the illusion of national purity. *Administrative Theory & Praxis* (M. E. Sharpe), *33*(1), pp. 62–79.

PART V

Who Am I Affecting?

12

MYSELF? OTHERS? HUMAN? NONHUMAN? IS THERE A DIFFERENCE?

THE ILLUSION OF "I"

I've come to the conclusion
That 'I' may be an illusion
Because all there is to see
Is not entirely me
This appearance can be changed
These thoughts rearranged
These organs can be replaced
This identity erased
And the spirit or soul . . .
Is untraceable in the whole
This breath needs air,
which is everywhere.
Once that starts to fade
'I' simply disintegrate
So 'I' am actually a fusion:
a blend, a mass collusion
What's supposed to be 'me':
Is nothing I can see
Therefore, in conclusion,
'I' must be an illusion

~ Joan Marques

The Challenge

It is not easy to convince people in a highly capitalistic society that there could be life after a single profit focus. The calls for more triple bottom line practices (considering people, planet, and profit), multilevel sustainability, and compassionate creativity may plant some positive seeds here and there, but still leave us too far away from an actual shift. This may be due to the fact that the community of believers in a constructive change, while growing, has not yet reached the scale to result in a tipping point. In other words, the idea of a world where we can perform and do well in a compassionate, responsible, sustainable, and multi-beneficial way has not yet reached the support level where it can weaken the dominance of the "Selfish Gain" mentality of the past centuries, and actually become a movement toward "Shared Growth."

The Continued Promotion of Selfish Gain

The single most powerful obstruction toward a real shift from selfish gain to shared growth is *perception*. Perception may sound like an internal thing, but it is oftentimes instilled externally, by surrounding factors such as our culture, education, religion, generation, and the environments in which we dwell and perform daily. In other words, our perception is shaped by the factors that influence us throughout our life. Some people have realized this and decided to be cautious on letting in too many external, troublesome influences. However, the majority of us are very receptive to perceptional influences. Thich Nhat Hanh (1991) describes our senses as windows to the world. He states, "Some of us leave our windows open all the time, allowing the sights and sounds of the world to invade us, penetrate us, and expose our sad, troubled selves" (p. 13).

The power of perception is immense and steadfast because it has multiple layers. To illustrate this, let us focus on three manifestations of perception. You should keep in mind, however, that there are many additional angles. The three perception-based areas on which we will focus here are: (1) social contradiction, (2) mental discrepancies, and (3) the high cost of moral performance.

Social Contradiction

Most human communities are full of contradictory compulsions. Older generations instill a number of mixed messages in upcoming ones, thereby not only confusing them but also forcing them to take a stance in favor of what is most rewarded. Till today, we practice the confusing way of formally promoting one behavior while actually rewarding its opposite. In a landmark article, Kerr (1975) presents a number of eye-opening examples about this contradictory trend as it is manifested in many layers and areas of human interaction. He refers to it as "rewarding A while hoping for B" (p. 769). Using politics as an example, Kerr discusses the reasons why political candidates remain vague about their goals in campaigns, even though the public demands specific ones. Why is that? Well, it is historically proven that when politicians actually adhere to public demand and present specific goals, they promptly get punished with a loss of votes. As an example of this contradiction in military service, Kerr (1975) reviews the Vietnam War, where soldiers would receive their reward of going back home as soon as their duty was over, regardless of the war's outcomes. Since the most assured way to get home was to stay out of danger, many soldiers did just that, and did not care about the governments' goal of winning the war.

Social contradictions are widespread and can be very costly, even to the extent of life endangering. Shifting the example of contradictions to human health, Kerr (1975) reveals why medical doctors prefer making the error of diagnosing healthy patients as seriously ill, instead of declaring them healthy and later finding that they were ill. The reason is that the punishment for declaring a sick person healthy far outstrips the one for declaring a healthy person sick, even though the latter often leads to great stress, devastation, and actual illness from side effects to superfluous medicines.

Kerr continues his review of social contradictions with the example of orphanages that claim to strive for placement of as many orphans as possible in good homes. Reality reveals, however, that they make the adoption procedures so strenuous that many decent potential parents get disheartened to even start the process. This contradictory practice is further supported by the fact that orphanages get their budgets on basis of the numbers of orphans in their homes, so there is an actual reward in keeping as many orphans in the orphanage as possible. In universities, explains Kerr, professors find that, contradictory to what society claims, their actual rewards are not based on being good teachers to their students, but on their research and publication records.

We can detect the contradiction in social behavior on a daily basis and in numerous realms. For instance, we teach people to be team players, but the recognition for individual achievement is far more attractive. We ask employees, departments, and services to be thrifty with their expenses, but reward those who exceed their budgets with larger sums of money next year, and punish those who were thrifty by shrinking their funds.

It is not difficult for workforce members to detect this tendency, and make up their minds about future moves: being irresponsible and uncaring about the common good seems to pay off more than the other way around. It takes a strong, morally mature mind, to do the right thing in spite of all the contradictory pressure.

Mental Discrepancies

We have all been young (some of the readers still are) and can therefore all relate to the mindset of being in our 20s or 30s. At this stage, we usually find ourselves on the fast track to "making it" at any cost, and do not care too much about those who suffer along the way, as long as our desires are met. Some people even keep this self-centered mindset at later stages in their lives, but there are also many who get painfully confronted with the fleetingness of everything. They may have lost dear ones, went through a divorce, suffered a major financial setback, endured a devastating layoff, or another crucible, and have come to the realization that continuous and selfish gathering only brings so much gratification, but cannot replace the most precious things in life.

In their book "True North," Bill George and Peter Sims (2007) mention numerous examples of leaders who found their true north after encountering crucibles. Among the leaders described is Howard Schulz, the Starbucks CEO and President, who learned from his father's misfortune of being laid off with a broken leg without any insurance or other incentive, that he would never do this to his employees if ever he would run his own corporation.

Yet, when we are still untouched by crucibles, we have a tendency to think we are invincible. A fellow researcher and I (Holt & Marques, 2012) did a longitudinal study with 87 undergraduate business students and 35 MBA students, and found that empathy was very lowly ranked among the undergraduate group, which comprised mostly younger students. This finding has been validated by several studies, which confirm that younger people generally have a lower capacity to feel empathy than older ones.

The High Cost of Moral Performance

It is no secret that many major corporations have long made up their mind on the aspect of immoral behavior, particularly in the case of harm to the environment. Watson (2010) finds that "while corporations [are] often quick to poison the environment, they tend to be very slow when it comes to fixing their mistakes" (par. 5). In reviewing the top-ten corporate payouts for environmental damage, Watson lists the huge amount British Petroleum had to pay for the 2010 spill in the Gulf of Mexico: $20 billion. However, the second largest amount, which was by Exxon, is a mere $3.5 billion, to which Watson concludes, "In most cases, the companies involved managed to reduce—or even erase—settlements through years of legal stalling and courtroom chicanery" (par. 7). Number three on Watson's list was Union Carbide, a corporate giant that ended up paying a scanty $470 million for the horrific Bhopal accident instead of the initially claimed $3 billion, with no option to prosecute the responsible management team due to the United States' refusal for extraditing the guilty parties to India, where the accident happened.

Indeed, recent history has shown us time and again that the fines companies have to pay when they have been caught in unethical behavior is far less than what they would pay if they would proactively apply morally sound and environmental safety measures in their operations. Kerr (1975) also focused on this trend in his earlier mentioned article. He found that if companies are placed before the choice of spending $11 million to purchase and install antipollution equipment versus not taking any preventive action and paying $1 million if caught in polluting the environment, most will go for the latter. This entails that a corporation will only do the right thing beforehand if its leaders and stockholders would be so morally driven that they would prefer to forego major profits and put themselves in an unfortunate position compared to their competitors. Since money is still the main driver of business ventures, this is not likely to happen.

Selfish Gains Summarized

As mentioned in the introductory statement of this section, the common factor of all the points made here is perception: perceptions in society, perceptions of upcoming generations, and perceptions of corporations and regulators. These are oftentimes externally imposed factors that numb the moral senses of those who fail to engage in thorough self-examination. There are undoubtedly more cases of perception maintaining the status quo, but the three angles presented previously demonstrate that we are dealing with a powerful and solid constellation of mental obstacles, which will not make it any easier to increase the support for an interconnected mindset.

The current state of performing and its supporting mechanisms, as described previously, are all elements of "modern" civilization, based on beliefs and behavioral patterns that have been developed and nurtured over the past centuries, and that will be hard to change. Hard, indeed, but not impossible. Why not impossible? Because human beings, while receptive to their environment, can also think and feel, and do so at a very personal, very internal level. We can reason and interpret the impressions our eyes convey to our brains. It requires willpower and a conscious mindset to understand that we have been treading down a path that has taken too high a toll thus far, and that we are gradually reaching the point where continuing on this path will only lead to our demise.

The Envisioned Path to Shared Growth

Whether you currently are or will end up running a major corporation or small venture, you cannot infinitely harvest without giving back. Resources are becoming depleted if we continue to gather at the current pace, environmental equilibriums get disrupted if we continue to pollute as we have been doing, and the antagonism of deprived groups will keep surging if we continue to brutally subjugate and take advantage of them. There have been writings on the wall in the past decade that should have warned us that it is time for something else: from the melting polar ice and the emergence of "terrorism" to repeated corporate scandals and downfalls.

We have been performing as caterpillars: consuming and gathering our way to growth, and expanding our sense of power, influence, and wealth, to a degree our forefathers never dreamed of. But caterpillars cease their acquisitive trend at a certain point, build a cocoon, and develop into butterflies for the next stage of their existence.

Humanity has reached that stage a while ago. While some of us may still want to behave as caterpillars, our time to develop into beautiful butterflies has come. We have to become more compassionate in our practices and give while we take, just like butterflies that flutter from flower to flower and use the nectar but also instigate cross-pollination at the same time.

We don't have to wait for society to change its contradictory signals, or for youngsters to start using their medial prefrontal cortex and obtain more social sensitivity, or for governments to increase fines for unethical corporate practices. We can simply relate, as leaders of ourselves and possibly others, to a number of simple notions, of which three will be reviewed subsequently.

The Realization of Interbeing

If we care to apply a mindful approach to all we do on a moment-to-moment basis, we can quickly detect the interbeing of everything; hence attain greater respect for all we are connected to. Thich Nhat Hanh (1991) explains interbeing in an easily understandable way. He uses the example of a piece of paper, which came from a tree, so the tree is in the paper. The tree needed the rain and the sun to grow, so the rain and sun are also in the paper. The rain came from a cloud, so the cloud is also in the paper. They all inter-are.

We can eat our breakfast and start contemplating on all the places where the various items we have in front of us come from and how many people and institutions, services, and organizations must have worked together to get it all here for our pleasure. We can review our clothes, our car, our appliances, and everything we use, and land at the same conclusion. A very effective way to increasingly understand and experience interbeing is through meditation. Referring to this path as "turning inward," Marques (2011) affirms that meditation can help reveal the following critical insights:

> 1) General awareness: the impermanence of everything; 2) Specific awareness: the fickleness of positions; 3) Holistic view: the ability to focus on the whole, and see past small irritations while recognizing the blessing of being where one is; 4) Learning Stance: the skill to understand that every seemingly negative occurrence serves a useful future purpose; 5) Interconnectedness: the connection with others, even if they refuse to see it; 6) Void: the awareness of one's non-self.
>
> *(p. 25)*

The Realization of Impermanence

In Marques' list of meditative revelations previously, impermanence was already mentioned. Indeed, by adopting a mindful approach, we can start to understand and internalize what is visible all around us: nothing lasts.

People, animals, plants, constructions, everything comes and goes. Nothing is permanent. We are all fleeting, and so are the systems we build, the wealth we gather, the powerful positions we acquire, and all the honors we accumulate. Nothing lasts eternally. This should not serve as a cue to stop performing and producing, but one that should help us temper our extreme orientations, expressed through insatiable tendencies.

What is more admirable than transcending the short-sighted "hit-and-run" mentality that so many business corporations adhere to, and exchanging it for a "give and take" pattern that ensures restoring as much as possible wherever our path leads us? Forests can be sustained by planting new trees when we harvest wood, local workers can be educated, so that they have a chance to develop themselves and their community at a higher level than before, and the abundant mentality in mining valuable gems can be tempered in order to decrease our carbon footprint. Nothing is everlasting. Not even our competitors. Many businesses do what they do because they fear that, if they don't, their competitors will surpass them. This is an assumption that is not void from truth. But why should we always compare ourselves to others? If history has taught us anything, it is that pioneers of laudable trends leave a lasting legacy. Is that not worth considering?

The Realization of Immaterial Happiness

Krishnamurti (N/A) once stated that he gained his inner balance and peace when he stopped comparing himself to others. In an interview posted on the official repository of the authentic teachings of J. Krishnamurti, he affirms

> Do you know what it means to live without psychological comparison when all your life you have been conditioned to compare—at school, at games, at the university and in the office? Everything is comparison. To live without comparison! Do you know what it means? It means no dependence, no self-sufficiency, no seeking, no asking; therefore it means to love. Love has no comparison, and so love has no fear. Love is not aware of itself as love, for the word is not the thing.
>
> *(par. 65)*.

Society encourages us continuously to compare ourselves to others, and oftentimes in an unfair way, which causes us to perceive ourselves as losers. Advertising is the best-known way in which this happens, and it is therefore also one of the swiftest ways to destroy our inner peace and dignity. You look at the models in magazines, and you instantly feel fat. You look at the brand-new car that can be leased for "only $495.00" a month, and yours instantly seems so out of date. You look at the clothes, workout machines, shoes, beds, food, jewelry, or new mobile phones that just came out, and you instantly feel as if yours are ready for the dump. The sad reality is, that we may experience instant gratification when we purchase all those advertised goods, or achieve those goals we formulated through comparison, but the happiness we gain from this is short-lived, because it is not really happiness. It is a superficial pacifier that temporarily numbs our dissatisfaction until the next challenge appears in this eternal comparison process.

Realizing that happiness is not acquired externally, but that it is a mental state that we can achieve through mindfulness is an important step toward lasting progress. Happiness is not encapsulated in a mansion on the hill or the newest make of a classy car: that's luxury. Happiness is not represented by inheriting a large sum of money or winning the lottery: that's luck, and within six months you are usually back to the state of mind that you had before. Happiness is not represented by a prestigious job, wealthy friends, and an impressive network: that's influence at the highest, and while it can be useful in climbing the corporate ladder or staying on top, it is not a substitute for happiness. Happiness is a by-product of mindfulness, when you realize that things could be so much worse; when you are aware of the blessings that are represented in the smallest things you encounter every day when you think on the things that are so easily overlooked: your health, your family, and your accomplishments today.

Shared Growth Summarized

The concepts of interbeing, impermanence, and immaterial happiness are very internal-based. Once we have reached the point where we dare to turn inward and face our interconnectedness with everything, they emerge as an interdependent cycle. Not everyone will care to turn inward and contemplate on these concepts, because it's easier to be ignorant. Ignorance numbs you when you engage in painful, wrong actions. Many people, some engaging in big business, are afraid to face their core because it may require them to make changes they dread making. Nonetheless, attaining a deeper understanding of these three interrelated phenomena will lead to greater inner peace. Attaining and maintaining inner peace may lead to giving up established behaviors, but why would we want to hold on to those if they were destructive anyway? At the end of every day, we have to face ourselves. Are we happy with our achievements of the day, or do we want to forget them as quickly as possible? If we are blessed, we will grow older. When looking back, will we be proud or embarrassed about our actions? We cannot take anything with us when our day of transition arrives. Why, then, should we gain at the expense and suffering of others with whom we inter are?

Shifting Gears: From Caterpillar to Butterfly

The driving motive for presenting the "Shared Growth" proposal mentioned previously can be found in an increasingly disturbing exhibition of the "Selfish Gain" tendency discussed earlier.

Using the analogy of a caterpillar and a butterfly, it is very important that we shift from the demanding, self-centered caterpillar stage to the reciprocal butterfly stage, thus ensuring longer and more rewarding existence of our species on this planet and a positive deposit on our collective emotional, ecological, and existential bank account.

References

George, B., & Sims, P. (2007). *True North: Discover Your Authentic Leadership*. Jossey-Bass, San Francisco, CA.

Hanh, T. N. (1991). *Peace Is Every Step: The Path of Mindfulness in Everyday Life*. Bantam Books, New York, NY.

Holt, S., & Marques, J. (2012). Empathy in leadership: Appropriate or misplaced? An empirical study on a topic that is asking for attention. *Journal of Business Ethics, 105*(1), pp. 95–105.

Kerr, S. (1975). On the folly of rewarding a, while hoping for b. *Academy of Management Journal, 18*(4), pp. 769–783.

Krishnamurti, J. (N/A). The urgency of change awareness. Retrieved May 25, 2013, from www.jkrishnamurti.org/krishnamurtiteachings/view-text.php?tid=5&chid=495.

Marques, J. (2011). Turning inward to connect outward: Interbeing as motivational path in today's workplace. *Interbeing, 5*(1), pp. 19–29.

Watson, B. (June 20, 2010). Corporate polluters: The 10 biggest environmental payouts. Retrieved May 25, 2013, from http://w ww.dailyfinance.com/2010/06/20/corporate—polluters-the-10-biggest-environmental-payouts/.

PART VI

What Matters in Leadership?

13

ON AWARENESS AND CONSCIOUSNESS

Reflection is a fairly simple activity, yet, many people forget to engage in it regularly. Frequent reflection can help us stay alert of our decisions because we dare to question them. It can also enable us to see the wider scope of our actions, and motivate us to reconsider first impulses. Reflection can help us understand that each choice we make is actually based on insufficient information, and that much of the course of our life depends on the actions we take after our decisions are made. What this means is that we may sometimes make poor decisions, but we can correct them if we reflect and find that the direction in which things are developing is unsatisfactory.

Wakeful leaders reflect in three dimensions: personal, relational, and professional.

- Personal reflection strengthens the relationship we have with ourselves. It can be achieved and maintained through self-imposed questions such as (a) how do I differ today from the person I was last year? (b) Have I changed for better or worse in moral regards? and (c) how can I (further) improve my moral performance from here onward?
- Relational reflection evaluates our connections with others and the nature of those connections. It can be practiced through insight enhancing contemplations such as: (a) what does this relationship mean to me? (b) What constructive actions have I taken in recent months to nurture this relationship? and (c) what constructive effects has this relationship had on me in recent months?
- Professional evaluation considers our connection with our formal activities. Some reflective questions we could ask in that regard are: (a) what am I passionate about professionally? (b) Is what I do today related to my passion? and (c) is my professional activity a constructive one to me and society? (Marques, 2015)

Allocating regular time to reflect helps us gain more influence of our past (because we get to appreciate it more), the present (because we experience it more intensely), and the future (because we consider it more deliberately). Self-reflection is a guaranteed way of staying mindful and preventing ourselves from mindless actions. Self-reflection is therefore not something we should only do once. It has to become a regular part of our life. Self-reflection can serve as a powerful thread that weaves our past, present, and future together: we see the bigger scheme better and realize that many of your setbacks are necessary parts in the puzzle that is our life. More importantly, self-reflection helps us make different decisions, based on broader considerations, thus elevating our moral and mental spectrum from merely the here and now, toward inclusion of the well-being of those that come after us.

Reference

Marques, J. F. (2015). Why wakeful leadership is more important now than ever. *Development and Learning in Organizations, 29*(3), pp. 18–20.

14

ON MINDFULNESS

OUR COMMON GROUND

There are no two moments alike
In this capricious journey of life
Ebbs and flows continuously strike
On this breathtaking, backbreaking hike
We so often fill with senseless strife

The art of living is no secret to us
We've been around long enough
We know that there's no fulfilment in fuss
It feels like riding in the wrong bus
On a road that's winding and rough

Yet, while all lessons were previously taught
We prefer to repeat old mistakes
The human path is inexplicably fraught
Through choices we make—promises we break
And directions we valiantly decide to take
Until by a surprising end we get caught . . .

What are we chasing, may I ask?
How do we perceive our personal trail?
What is, in the end, our critical task?

> And what are we hiding behind our mask?
> Are we the hammer and is life our nail?
>
> Acquiring peace is a personal choice
> Regardless of the turmoil around
> We can find tranquility amidst noise
> Discover our inner peace-loving poise
> And make mutual acceptance our common ground
> ~ *Joan Marques*

Mindfulness is critical for everyone who aims to increase a positive atmosphere and a sense of connection in a workplace (Petchsawang & Duchon, 2012). When you practice mindfulness, you will experience greater mental presence, which will help you connect better with others and engage more fully in your job (Federman, 2009). Today we find mindfulness training programs in several major workplaces such as Google, the US Army, and Harvard Business School (Petchsawang & McLean, 2017).

As I indicated in a previous section, nurturing a detached mindset in your workplace can help you reduce a sense of aversion and hurt, while it will also bring to the forefront the need to be mindful and understand that everything in life comes and goes anyway Metcalf and Hately (2001). Morvay (1999) uses the term "healthy detachment," tying it into the practice of mindfulness, and explaining that being mindful can help us realize that we are open and receptive onlookers toward the ordinary stream of consciousness without preconception or judgment. Ghose (2004) also reminds us that Buddhist psychology strongly relies on the practice of mindfulness as the foundation of all actions and decisions. Thich Nhat Hanh (1976) underscores in that regard that all our feelings, whether positive or negative, strong or weak, should be considered with mindfulness, since this is what protects our psyche from harm.

Engaging in mindfulness practice could lead to positive changes in our lives and the lives of those around us, as it may enhance our collective insights into responsible and moral conduct toward all that exists. Foundational Buddhist implementation of mindfulness is inseparably linked to ethical conduct. It meticulously observes the Buddhist five precepts of non-killing, non-stealing, no sexual misconduct, no wrongful speech, and non-partaking in alcohol and drugs as part of mindfulness practice (Murphy, 2016). In several Western-developed mindfulness exercises, these concepts are disregarded, which may leave the door open to mindfulness without moral foundation. While therefore admitting to the enormous benefits in mindfulness training for non-Buddhist audiences, Murphy (2016) also warns for the possibility of a misinterpretation and malpractice of mindfulness, void of the Buddhist concepts of non-harming, morality, loving–kindness, and compassion. She also raises the cautionary reasoning that mindfulness training can be presented in an overly positive light, thus downplaying abusive practices such as turning a blind eye to potential negative outcomes of this practice.

Van Gordon et al. (2017) also advocate the Buddhist meditative practice of mindfulness as the one that will cultivate important foundational concepts of compassion, loving–kindness, and moral responsibility. With that, they also support Thich Nhat Hanh's (1998) notion that true aptitude in mindfulness requires not only awareness of the present moment but also a solid understanding of the true and absolute (self-less) mode in which the present moment exists. It is therefore prudent to underscore the necessity of including the moral aspect of mindfulness practice, which we could refer herewith as "mindful mindfulness."

The Intersection of Mindfulness and Awareness

Awareness should not be confused with mindfulness. Awareness is a foundational quality of what was referred to above as "mindful mindfulness." Awareness should not be confused with attention either. Rapgay and Bystrisky (2009) clarify in that regard that attention denotes an every-changing factor of consciousness, while awareness pertains to a stable and specific state of consciousness as well as a function. When considered a function, awareness is more an introspective or observational sensation that monitors experiences. When considered as a state, awareness refers to the nature of consciousness. The nature of consciousness is expansive and is capable of containing a variety of experiences (Rapgay & Bystrisky, 2009). Berkhin and Hartelius (2011) also describe awareness as a function, informing us that Buddhist practice is focused on meanings rather than events, and the meanings are instilled by moment-by-moment awareness of our condition. Sundararajan (2008) identifies reflexivity and second-order awareness, whereby reflexivity awareness pertains to the knowledge or insight in what we already know, while second-order awareness (as opposed to first-order experience) pertains to a higher level consciousness, whereby we have an experience, and then an experience of that experience.

Below are some important reminders for those of us who would like to practice mindfulness:

1. Being mindful is not a one-time project. It requires ongoing effort because it can evaporate so easily when we settle into our activities, work- or lifestyles. Fortunately, mindfulness can be polished regularly, for instance through meditation, or through regular scanning of your thoughts (Junttila, N/A), and asking yourself whether you are being mindful or are being mindless. The more you ask yourself that question, the more deliberate your actions will become, and the fewer mindless moments you will have.

2. Life is a continuous sequence of mindfulness disruptions, which may come in many forms: problems at home or work, relationship issues, loss or illness, which can give rise to old bad habits, distract you from your mindfulness efforts (Junttila), thus propelling you back into sleepwalking mode.

3. The many distractions and setbacks in work and private life may cause your mindfulness efforts to stall regularly or progress so slowly that you get discouraged (Junttila). Of course, setbacks are the best opportunities to prove your determination and test your mindfulness. But that is easier said than done.

4. Your goals may infringe on your mindfulness efforts (Junttila). You may get so geared up about reaching a goal that you suddenly realize that you have placed your mindfulness efforts on hold, and have fallen into many of your old sleepwalking habits. Goals are great, but they can also be powerful distractions to remaining mindful.

5. Achieving your goals may cause another major infringement on your mindfulness (Junttila). If you reach a goal and don't set a new one, you run the chance of becoming languid, and losing the zest to move on. Lethargy is one of the major drivers of mindlessness. Lack of activity equals lack of purpose, and that equals lack of a reason to nourish mindfulness.

6. Dreading your current circumstances can also become an obstacle toward mindfulness. It may lead to depression and rob you from the will to focus. However, dreadful situations are also a great opportunity for sharpening your mindfulness efforts and understanding the purpose of the current moment in the wholeness of your life (Junttila).

References

Berkhin, I., & Hartelius, G. (2011). What altered states are not enough: A perspective from Buddhism. *International Journal of Transpersonal Studies*, *30*(1–2), pp. 63–68.

Federman, B. (2009). *Employee Engagement: A Roadmap for Creating Profits, Optimizing Performance, and Increasing Loyalty*. Jossey-Bass, San Francisco, CA.

Ghose, L. (2004). A study in Buddhist psychology: Is Buddhism truly pro-detachment and anti-attachment? *Contemporary Buddhism*, *5*(2), pp. 105–120.

Hanh, T. N. (1976). *The Miracle of Mindfulness*. Beacon Press, Boston, MA.

Hanh, T. N. (1998). *The Heart of the Buddha's Teaching: Transforming Suffering Into Peace, Joy, and Liberation*. Broadway Books, New York, NY.

Junttila, H. (N/A). 7 Obstacles to mindfulness and how to overcome them. *TinyBuddha.com*. Retrieved from http://tinybuddha.com/blog/7-obstacles-to-mindfulness-and-how-to-overcome-them/.

Metcalf, F., & Hately, B. G. (2001). *What Would Buddha Do at Work?* Seastone and Berrett-Koehler Publishers, Inc., San Francisco, CA.

Morvay, Z. (1999). Horney, Zen, and the real self: Theoretical and historical connections. *American Journal of Psychoanalysis*, *59*(1), pp. 25–35.

Murphy, A. (2016). Mindfulness-based therapy in modern psychology: Convergence and divergence from early Buddhist thought. *Contemporary Buddhism*, *17*(2), pp. 275–325.

Petchsawang, P., & Duchon, D. (2012). Workplace spirituality, meditation, and work performance. *Journal of Management, Spirituality & Religion, 9*(2), pp. 189–208.

Petchsawang, P., & McLean, G. N. (2017). Workplace spirituality, mindfulness meditation, and work engagement. *Journal of Management, Spirituality & Religion, 14*(3), pp. 216–244.

Rapgay, L., & Bystrisky, A. (2009). Classical mindfulness. *Annals of the New York Academy of Sciences, 1172*, pp. 148–162.

Sundararajan, L. (2008). Toward a reflexive positive psychology: Insights From the Chinese Buddhist notion of emptiness. *Theory & Psychology, 18*(5), pp. 655–674.

Van Gordon, W., Shonin, E., & Griffiths, M. D. (2017). Buddhist emptiness theory: Implications for psychology. *Psychology of Religion and Spirituality, 9*(4), pp. 309–318.

15

ON ATTITUDE

Sometime, somewhere, I read the following mind-bending, thought-swirling, brain-sticking statement, "We don't see things as they are; we see them as we are." That's not just perception at work. The real characteristic that triggers it all here is . . . attitude.

Our attitude determines the lion share of how we experience our lives. You may have heard or read this before: "We should see problems as opportunities." And sure enough: If we would replace the word "problem" with "opportunity" every time we encounter one, it would be amazing how we could influence our approach toward any issue. Statements such as "making lemonade from the lemons life throws at us" or "laying a firm foundation with the bricks others throw at us" are exactly focused on that: helping us realize that our attitude can be a lifesaver or a destructive force.

For yes: lemons and bricks will be thrown at us by life's happenstances and by some people we encounter along the way. Sometimes the mental lemons and bricks will be for real, and sometimes they will seem that way due to our experiences. Whether it's at work, home, or at social meetings, we could always find something to bring us down; may it be a treatment, a comment, a look, a seemingly degrading grin, or our own general feeling of insecurity and discomfort.

The problem with attitudes manifests itself in every layer and environment of society. Ochalla et al. (2002) explain, for instance, that "[m]any business professionals are unaware of the attitude they convey. While they may be doing all the physical things correctly—such as giving firm handshakes, correctly saying the client's name and dressing appropriately—their attitude sabotages their business success." Ochalla, Gall, and Casperson then mention issues such as lack of respect, being preoccupied, interrupting clients, displaying nervous or annoying mannerisms, and using unfavorable speech patterns.

The aforementioned is just a detail of the attitudinal theme. The broader scope is even more compelling. It deals with everything that happens to us. It deals with life in general and what we make of it. Most of the problems we experience on a daily basis can be shifted into opportunities or useful lessons if we just care to adjust our attitude. No everything that seems good is really good, and similarly, not everything that seems bad is actually bad. Sometimes we find out in hindsight, that a great opportunity arrived disguised as a challenge.

Some of the lessons I have learned from the bricks that were thrown at me are:

- The more you run and push, the less will happen. This doesn't mean that you should rest on your laurels and refrain from taking any initiative; but it does mean that panic and devastation are not the feelings in place when things are delicate. It has to do with switching your mindset into a conviction that everything you lose, just makes place for something better that's coming up. Not an easy thought to hold on to when everything seems to squeeze you where it hurts most. But an extremely valuable one once you start believing in it. One of my role models in life told me in one of the darkest career hours I experienced in the past period, "God never closes a door without at least opening a window." And to be honest, it may take some time before you see that window—but as long as you believe it's there, you'll see it.
- Readiness to act positively but alert upon circumstances is priceless. If you haven't read the book "Who Moved My Cheese" (Johnson & Blanchard, 1998) yet, you need to do so. It teaches you the a–b–c of attitude in action: not taking anything for granted, but hanging your running shoes around your neck, no matter how great the current situation looks. After all, one never knows when it will be time to run again, right? Getting great opportunities means, being there—and ready—when they are presented.
- Seeming setbacks can turn out to be mere disguises for great opportunities in hindsight. Being laid off from your current workplace may require temporary financial strictness, but in the long run, it may lead to the dream job and the star performance you always cherished. Rest assured that if they think that letting you go is a wise thing to do, they are not worth your efforts and devotion anyway. Recognition will come, most likely from an unexpected corner—soon! Just remain ready and open-minded.
- Opportunity can knock in strange ways and at unexpected times. That ties in with keeping the open mind I just mentioned. Don't narrow the mental picture you have of your capacities to just one area. You can do more than you think. And you can apply your skills in far more areas than you would hold for possible!
- Look at everything from the most positive angle you can find. Think of the power of perception, which we all can learn to master if we choose. It's the theme Frederick Langbridge captured so well in his statement, "two men look out the same prison bars; one sees mud and the other stars," and what

Emerson meant when he once said, "to different minds, the same world is a hell, and a heaven." What one perceives as a straight disaster, another sees as a chance to prove himself.

• Maintain an attitude of suitable pride and progress, in spite of the many hurdles that will be laid on your path, in the shape of money (or the lack thereof), race, gender, sexual preference, looks, or even the neighborhood where you happen to live! Yet, don't be overly proud and excessively confident either. Remain flexible as the grass, so that you can bend, and not sturdy as the tree that can be uprooted in a hard wind.

In his bestselling book "Man's Search for Meaning," Victor E. Frankl (2006) made a number of immortal statements. But maybe the most unforgettable one was that everything can be taken from a man or a woman but one thing: the last of human freedoms—to choose one's attitude in any given set of circumstances, to choose one's own way. And wasn't Frankl right? While we cannot change our past, future, or even the present, we can choose how we want to look at and deal with it. This is where the key to survival and success lies.

Our attitude is undoubtedly our most important business card to the world, but even more, to ourselves!

References

Frankl, V. E. (2006). *Man's Search for Meaning.* Beacon Press, New York, NY.

Johnson, S., & Blanchard, K. (1998). *Who Moved My Cheese?* G. P. Putnam's Sons, New York, NY.

Ochalla, B., Gall, K., & Casperson, D. M. (April 2002). *Getting It Done: Improve Your Attitude.* Credit Union Management, Madison.

16

ON AUTHENTICITY

Authenticity has to do with being genuine, factual, and honest. It matters both internally and externally, but it is more complicated than it seems at first. You may think that it is easier to know your authentic self, because no one knows the real you better than you, right? Still, the demands of contemporary life can place so much pressure on your idea of who you are that it is easy to get trapped into thinking that you are what is merely a passing stage of your existence: a position, a relationship, a cultural, or other type of affinity, to name some examples. Yet, your authentic self goes far beyond the skin-deep level. It has to do with your spiritual core and is a journey of discovery that you regularly have to undertake. Authenticity toward the external world is not a holiday either, especially when you perform in different settings that demand different behaviors from us. Your position as a manager at work requires specific behavioral cues as compared to your task as a member of your church, the head of your family, or the child of your parents.

When you attempt to respond honestly and openly to others, without pretenses, and with full respect for their existence, you are making a good effort toward authentic behavior. "You don't learn to walk by following rules. You learn by doing, and by falling over," says Sir Richard Branson (2014). Branson, best known for the Virgin brand, makes a very authentic impression. He is sympathetic, accepts his shortcomings, communicates with great ease with people from all walks of life, and seems to celebrate life one day at a time.

Bill George (2003), who has written and taught extensively on the topic, explains authentic leadership as "driven by passion and purpose, not greed" (p. 6). It is George's opinion that "there are five essential dimensions to authentic leaders: purpose, values, heart, relationships, and self-discipline" (p. 6). George (2003) perceives authentic leadership as "the only way to build lasting value [by focusing] on the company's missions, customers, and employees" (p. 30). He also feels that authenticity in performance gets best maintained when you focus on the people around you, and the goal you are collectively trying to achieve. George considers it important to connect with stakeholders on a daily basis, because that is the most rewarding way for defining positive growth for all. He also invites us to regularly examine our core values, and then consider whether what we do is still in line with those values. The people around us quickly pick up on that behavior and will have great respect if they realize that their leader remains true to his or her values. Chances are that they will mirror that practice, and also develop into authentic leaders.

Bonau (2017) agrees that authenticity is a crucial trait for inspirational leaders. She stresses that, while not all authentic leaders may be inspirational in nature, it remains a fact that leaders would not be able to genuinely inspire followers if they were not true to their values and goals. Bonau stresses that authentic leaders are a greater asset to humanity as a whole, due to the positive development they aspire to bring, than inauthentic leaders.

Zbierowski (2016) describes authenticity as a foundational element in positive leadership theories. He explains authenticity as a combination of owning our personal experiences and acting in accordance with our true self. Within that scope, honesty and openness are primary prerequisites, because these qualities serve as major encouragers for a good understanding and optimal team spirit. Other characteristics that have been attributed to authentic leadership are confidence, hope, optimism, resilience, transparency, ethics, future orientation, and connectivity (Luthans & Avolio, 2003).

It is particularly Bill George's suggestion of regularly examining whether your decisions and actions are still in line with your values that captures the art and practice of authenticity. It is, however, equally important to comment that we are organic beings, and that our perspectives, and yes, even some of our values, may change over time, as we witness developments and obtain insights we did not have before. Once we learn that some of our prior ideas were shortsighted or based on ill-informed traditions, we may also find that our "authentic" self-changes, and that we no longer support our now obsolete mindsets. That, too, is a practice that we should respect in ourselves, and consider part of the dynamic beings we are in a world that is constantly changing, and where we can only try to be the best person we are at any given time.

References

Bonau, S. (2017). How to become an inspirational leader, and what to avoid. *Journal of Management Development, 36*(5), pp. 614–625.

Branson, R. (2014). You learn by doing and by falling over. Retrieved from www.virgin.com/richardbranson/you-learn-doing-and-falling-over.

George, B. (2003). Authentic leadership. *CMA Management, 77*(8), p. 6.

Luthans, F., & Avolio, B. (2003). Authentic leadership development. In K. S. Cameron, J. E. Dutton, & R. E. Quinn (Eds.), *Positive Organizational Scholarship. Foundations of a New Discipline* (pp. 241–258). Berrett-Koehler Publishers, San Francisco, CA.

Zbierowski, P. (2016). Positive leadership and corporate entrepreneurship: Theoretical considerations and research propositions. *Entrepreneurial Business and Economics Review*, 4(3), pp. 73–84.

17

ON MENTAL MODELS

Mental models are our internal pictures of how the world works. Because our mental models are our own deeply ingrained ideas about the world around us, influenced by our upbringing, education, culture, ethnic background, religion, and other determining factors, they often form a major hurdle in accepting new ways of thinking and acting. If we are unaware of our mental models—and many people are—they can severely debilitate how we perceive the world.

Peter Senge (1992), who is a prominent thinker and author on mental models, explains, "Mental models can be simple generalizations, such as 'people are untrustworthy', 'or they can be complex theories'. But what is most important to grasp is that mental models shape how we act. If we believe people are untrustworthy, we act differently from the way we would if we believed they were trustworthy."

In striving to do the right thing as leaders of ourselves and others, it is important to understand how mental models work and what they do: they are represented in the stories we believe and the assumptions we hold. Because we take them for granted and assume they are the only way reality can be considered, our mental model's shape—and can often distort—our interpretation of external impulses. Therefore, it may happen that two people listen to the same statement, yet, one hears a compliment, while the other hears an insult. Mental models don't just differ among people from different backgrounds or cultures: sometimes people from the same family or circle of friends can have very differing mental models. This is because our characters, personal experiences, and mindsets also play a major role in the shaping of our mental models.

Once we become aware of them, we should also notice that our mental models are highly imperfect. They are limited, unbalanced, and are often irrational and miserly. Yet, they evolved as a natural process: through our interactions with other people and a variety of situations. Human beings need to require their mental models because they provide simplified explanations to complex situations. We develop behavioral patterns on basis of our mental models. We develop beliefs about how our devices work, for instance, and take extra measures because of those beliefs. If your computer is frequently crashing, then you may develop the mental model of shutting it down in a particular way to prevent another crash. When you purchase a new computer, you may apply the same mental model to this new machine, even if unnecessary and outdated. While our mental models enable us to filter the abundance of information that comes to us and helps us determine our stance with more ease and make quicker decisions, they may be inaccurate and withhold us from new paths and possibilities that could be advantageous.

In most Western nations, such as the United States, people are taught that an individualistic mindset is the natural way for human beings to perform. A focus on self-progress and selfish gain, even if at the expense of others, is therefore highly preferred. This self-focus has even grown into a societal addiction, oftentimes creating a series of ignorant behaviors in personal and professional environments. Selfish gain is generally rewarded because accumulating wealth or profits is a sign of having understood the dominant mental model. This shows that mental models, or perceptions, are not always internally created, but very often prompted by signals from our environment.

Some of the social factors that can influence our mental models are:

1. Social contradiction: Most human communities are full of contradictory forces. Previous generations exert mixed messages to younger ones by rewarding exactly those things that they claim should be avoided or punished. You can even see this at both personal and professional levels. In personal regards, we are told to nurture a team spirit, but often find that individual performance is more abundantly rewarded. In professional regards, many business and government departments quickly understand that they should never try to stay under last year's budget, even if they are told to do so. Remaining under budget means that next year's budget will be reduced. Going over the limits ensures a larger budget for next year.

2. Mental inconsistencies: Our paradigms shift as we mature. At younger ages, we usually don't care too much about others and try to achieve our goals at any cost. As we mature, we gradually start to understand that there is more to life than making money: we have then been confronted with the crucibles of life, and have learned that happiness is made up of different factors.

3. The price of moral performance: This often manifests itself in the business world. Doing the right thing usually costs much more and requires a tremendous amount of effort compared to risking a fine. The fine is usually tens or even hundreds of times cheaper than proper behavior. The unwritten rule is, therefore: go ahead and take the chance, and we'll see what happens if we

get caught. A sad example of this trend is the Union Carbide Corporation (I also shared this example in a previous chapter), which was responsible for a major gas leak in India in 1984, whereby more than a half million people were exposed to dangerous chemicals, resulting in an immediate death toll of 2,259 souls. The company only paid $470 million instead of the initially demanded $3 billion, without an option to prosecute the responsible management team, because the United States refused to extradite the guilty managers to India, where the accident had transpired.

It is critical to understand that we harbor mental models because it can help us in becoming aware of the fact that other people view things differently from the way we do. Knowing about our mental models also helps us to understand how often we are wrong due to our limited view. It can help us to cease our attempts to prove others wrong, because we become more aware of our own limitations in seeing, reasoning, and concluding. Most importantly, knowing about our mental models can encourage us to rethink them and change them in areas where they make us miserable. Below are some suggestions for proactive measures to change potentially damaging mental models:

1. Active note-taking: This may require some self-discipline, but walking around with a pen and notebook and actively taking notes of your beliefs. When reviewing them, you will find which ones come from your upbringing, and which ones are new. Then you can decide which ones to change and which to keep.
2. Meditation: This is an effective strategy toward changing mental models. There are several ways of meditating, so it's left to the meditator to decide how, when, and where he wants to practice this exercise. Vipassana meditation is also known as mindfulness meditation or insight meditation. While it is often associated with Buddhism, some sources maintain that it existed even before the Buddhist philosophy was developed. Vipassana is a practice of turning inward to gain insight into one's existence, the workings of cause and effect, and the destructive workings of mental biases. Practicing Vipassana meditation awakens us to the impermanence of everything, including our own impermanence. As we become familiar with that awareness, we also become aware of the futility of entitlement, pettiness, holding grudges, and other negative emotions. Vipassana raises our awareness of the damage that both craving and aversion have done to us. In the next chapter, we will elaborate some more on this meditation technique.
3. Practice of interbeing. Thich Nhat Hanh (1991), one of the world's most revered and well-known Buddhist monks (cited earlier in this book), coined the term "interbeing" and explained it this way: "If you are a poet, you will see clearly that there is a cloud floating in this sheet of paper. Without a cloud, there will be no rain; without rain, the trees cannot grow; and

without trees, we cannot make paper. The cloud is essential for the paper to exist. If the cloud is not here, the sheet of paper cannot be here either. So we can say that the cloud and the paper inter-are. "Interbeing" is a word that is not in the dictionary yet, but if we combine the prefix "inter-" with the verb "to be," we have a new verb, inter-be." Just like with Vipassana, the concept of interbeing is not intended from any religious or poetic angle, but from a pure realistic standpoint. When we take the time to think on our dependence on others, and how all we are is the collective input from so many factors, we awaken from the narrow mindset of "I," "me," and "mine." Thanks to this realization, we no longer cling to things and end our suffering of attachment and aversion.

References

Hanh, T. N. (1991). *Peace Is Every Step: The Path of Mindfulness in Everyday Life*. Bantam Books, New York, NY.

Senge, P. M. (1992). Mental models. *Planning Review, 20*(2), p. 4.

18

ABOUT SLEEPWALKING

When the term "sleepwalking" is used, many people may think of someone walking in their sleep, stereotypically with stretched arms and closed eyes. In this chapter, we do not refer to that type of sleepwalking. Within the leadership perspective of this chapter, sleepwalking pertains to the many mindless acts we perform on a daily, weekly, monthly, or even yearly basis, without wondering about them. It's about implementing habitual patterns without questioning whether they still matter, and about staying in situations—personal or professional—that have long ago lost their luster to us. It's about walking, talking, acting, and deciding without critical or creative thinking.

Once the above is taken into consideration, we cannot escape the awareness that many people sleepwalk with their eyes wide open. They are everywhere: the colleague that has been complaining for 10 years now about her job, but has not done anything to pursue a more rewarding career; the sister who's been dreading her marriage, but doesn't want to consider taking a leap toward her own happiness because she would be the first in the family to divorce; the brother who keeps feeling sorry for himself, because of all the chances he missed in the past; or the friend who remains stuck in his old routine, even though it stopped satisfying him years ago. When reflecting deeply, we will all be able to identify some sleepwalk patterns in our own behavior.

Sleepwalking is the opposite of being awake. People who sleepwalk, move through the motions of personal and professional life without questioning whether they still matter to them. Human beings have a tendency of becoming mindless and do things either because they have done them for a long time, or because they were done this way for a long time. Mindless continuation of traditions is an often occurring form of sleepwalking. Something was once done this way, and nobody wonders whether it still has a purpose today (Marques, 2014).

Some forms of sleepwalking are even brought within religious or cultural realms, making them even harder to challenge or change. Some people go to their church or temple two or three times a week, simply because the tradition has been set that way for decades. Unfortunately, they don't even pay attention to what their pastor or preacher says. Once out of their religious home, they live like savages with each other, mistrusting and insulting each other, unwilling to support any social cause, and filled with senses of discrimination, greed, and hatred. These are all serious forms of sleepwalking.

Some cultures prohibit their offspring from dating and marrying outside the racial or cultural boundaries. Youngsters who choose to oppose this rule get disowned and possibly even abandoned from their family or the entire community. Protection of the ethnic purity is so important to them that it overbears any common or humane sense. And mindlessly, the tradition is observed year after year, decade after decade, without ever considering the bigger picture of human interconnectedness.

Sleepwalking has a lot to do with focusing too much on the details and forgetting to zoom out in order to obtain a broader scope. Discrimination of any kind is also a form of sleepwalking: it is an act that is based on superficial differences, mostly external or acquired, without considering the many overarching commonalities. Those who discriminate hold beliefs that they are somehow better than others, either because of their race, culture, education, age, status, or another parameter they erected and labeled as important. The mindset these discriminating folks nurture was most likely adopted from previous generations without any screening or critical reflection about its purpose, sense, or origins (Marques, 2014).

Racism and prejudice have been particular topics of interest in recent years, and the word is out that these forms of sleepwalking are to be attributed to a lower IQ (Pappas, 2012). Studies have revealed that there seems to be a vicious cycle at play here, where individuals with lower intelligence levels gravitate more to conservative trends, resist change, and are more prone to develop attitudes of prejudice. It is important to emphasize that the study findings pertain to large groups and that there are definitely exceptions in every group (Pappas, 2012), in other words, not every person who holds conservative notions has a lower IQ, and not every liberal has a higher IQ. Yet, people who are more closed toward changes and "different ways of thinking" seem to suffer, on average, from lower intelligence levels, which disable them to place themselves in the place of those who are the subject of their prejudice.

Ending the sleepwalk habit begins with realizing that it is there: that we are a product of our environment, and that we have been shaped by the stimuli we were exposed to over the past decades: our upbringing, culture, religion, peers, teachers, perhaps even our ethnic group, neighborhood, generation, or workplace. Any source that impacted us over the years has contributed to the person we are today, thus, the perceptions we hold of "reality," and the decisions we make. It is important to consider also, that it is easier to sleepwalk than to keep oneself awake! It is also easy to regress into the sleepwalking habit again after having been "awakened" and having made some bold decisions.

Effects of Sleepwalking

As can be derived from the section mentioned previously, sleepwalking can lead to a lot of trouble, not only for the person who sleepwalks but also for those who get affected by this behavior. In the case of racism, for instance, the racist may not even suffer as much from his or her behavior as those who are subjected to the act. Oftentimes, however, sleepwalkers experience the disadvantages of their ways. Refusing to change is almost always equal to falling behind, especially in these times of continuous change.

It should be understood why sleepwalking is such a widespread phenomenon. It is because human beings, by default, are creatures of habit, hence, change averse. We love to dwell in our comfort zones, and that is understandable to a great extend: once we have developed a pattern, it is just easier to follow the same trend repeatedly. It requires less mental energy to find our way through our routine. It is like performing on autopilot. But there are limits to everything: performing on autopilot for too long can derail our focus on new trends, and new trends keep emerging, whether we like it or not. Especially in professional circles, it will be self-destructive to behave like a sleepwalker.

Still, people fall prey to this mindless trend. They often make choices that feel good at one time, and then fail to keep track of the changes around them, and even those that happen within! Many people cannot understand their own change process. If they liked what they did once, how can they dislike it today? If they made such a deliberate decision to be where they currently are, how can it seem so unpleasant or unsuitable today? Of course, the answer is not too hard to retrieve: everything changes. Nothing is permanent. We live in a world where even our life is not infinite, let alone our relationships or professional circumstances. We are in constant flux and regularly move up and down the ladder of progress. There is no guarantee that the trend will always be upward. Those who have experienced the economic downturn of 2008 can attest to that. Many people lost jobs that they thought would be theirs for the rest of their professional life. From one day to another, they had to give up their prestigious homes and some even became homeless. If there is one thing that doesn't change it is the fact that life is unpredictable. Because of this unpredictability, we owe it to ourselves to remain mindful and refrain from sleepwalking.

Regardless of the measures we take to safeguard our life and circumstances, we don't have the ability to ensure that our life will be a smooth ride. And when we review challenges from this angle, we may be able to see their purpose: they shake us at our core and force us to refocus. If only for a short while, we snap out of the sleepwalking habit and understand the need to think creatively.

Thinking creatively is an immediate consequence of mindfulness, which will be discussed next in this chapter). As we become more alert of the shifting conditions of things around us, we realize that old solutions will not effectively solve new challenges. Our chance of success increases tremendously when we apply creativeness and stop doing what everybody else does (Nissley, 2009). As an example, when we lose one job, we should be mindful in looking for another one in exactly the same field. This is what most people do. They try to recapture the same routine, even if they are forced to do it elsewhere. Instead of doing this, they could consider the disconnect from their prior work and habit pattern as an encouragement to explore a different path.

One Princeton college graduate who applied mindfulness in the midst of the 2008 economic downturn realized that his college degree was not going to help him in the dire circumstances he encountered upon returning home. He laid aside his previous intentions of becoming a major executive in a large corporation, scanned his hometown for local needs, and started a worm farm to make nutrient-rich compost for gardeners. Because so many businesses had closed, he could find cheap warehouse space for rent, and started collecting scraps from restaurants. "He surely didn't get a degree in worm farming, but he thought up an idea and made it work" (Nissley, 2009).

Individuals are not the only ones who sleepwalk. Organizations fall prey to this problematic behavior as well. This is understandable because organizations are run by people, and if the people driving the organization are unaware or unwilling to apply necessary changes, the organization may land in an indolent situation that will harm its competitiveness and general performance and growth. There are numerous examples of businesses that once thrived but lost their edge due to sleepwalking (e.g., Blockbuster, Eastman Kodak, Motorola, Sony, Toys "R" Us). Within the organizational context, sleepwalking is usually equal to lack of innovation. Some major business corporations such as General Motors and Ford, once the biggest and most prestigious car companies on the globe, have been losing market share and profits due to their failure to keep up with younger generations of automakers.

Some of the most common reasons why individuals fell into the sleepwalking trap are the following:

- They feel that thinking is a passive pursuit. They claim that they are too busy to make the time for sitting and thinking. And that, while there's nothing lazy or passive about thinking.
- They confine their thinking to their current field of action, or they have learned to think within the boundaries of their daily environment.
- At work, they are not rewarded for creative thinking. There are still many work environments—and bosses—who can get very displeased with out-of-the-box thinkers or healthy risk takers.
- They may also be subject to peer pressure, sometimes even unconsciously. Especially those of us who are very close with our family or friends may want

approval from them, but if they are traditionalists, they will not encourage anything out of the ordinary, or anything that may require you to move away.

- They may face self-imposed blockades, which so many people maintain, such as self-esteem issues, or fear for what others may think of them, which prohibits them from wading into areas outside of their mental comfort zone (Lavine, 2009).
- They are subjected to a highly routine-based (mechanistic) environment, which does not encourage critical thinking, because the actions to be applied are highly repetitive. This is why we often see telephone operators, checkout clerks, and airline personnel sleepwalk through their days, mechanically fulfilling the tasks that were outlined for them (Langer & Moldoveanu, 2000).
- They may come from cultures or living environments where mindfulness was punished, or where mindless following was rewarded (King & Sawyer, 1998).

The effect of sleepwalking on business entities is decline unless they manage to reinvent themselves and come up with a product or service that restores their position in their field. The effect of sleepwalking for human beings could be considered similar: we, too, can first fall off the bandwagon, but then wake up, and come up with a way to reinvent ourselves in order to return to the point of fulfillment or prestige we desire. That's the beauty of being alive and thinking: regardless of our mistakes, we can correct them and move on, sometimes even better than before.

However, when we are in sleepwalk mode, we may not think too deeply about it, but we usually feel depressed, and it is no secret what depression can do to us. Being unfulfilled and unhappy for long periods of time reduces our patients and can turn us into moody, grouchy people. Healthwise, it can cause us to acquire high blood pressure, push us toward destructive habits such as alcohol, drug abuse, or overeating, and possibly lead to a stroke, a heart attack, or other psychosomatically driven diseases.

On the other hand, mindful performance keeps us fulfilled, even though it would be foolish to think that every day will be at an equal high. Even wakeful people experience downs sometimes because life is happening to them as well. They just don't allow these setbacks to get the best of them, and bounce back much quicker than sleepwalkers do. Overall, the quality of their life is therefore at a much higher level.

References

King, P. E., & Sawyer, C. R. (1998). Mindfulness, mindlessness and communication instruction. *Communication Education, 47*(4), pp. 326–336.

Langer, E., & Moldoveanu, M. (2000). The construct of mindfulness. *Journal of Social Issues, 56*(1), pp. 1–9.

Lavine, D. S. (March 16, 2009). Creative thinking. *National Law Journal, 31*(28), p. 13.

Marques, J. (2014). *Leadership and Mindful Behavior: Action, Wakefulness, and Business*. Palgrave-Macmillan, New York, NY.

Nissley, E. L. (March 29, 2009). *Creative Thinking Goes Long Way*. McClatchy—Tribune Business News originally posted by The Times-Tribune, Scranton, PA.

Pappas, S. (January 26, 2012). Low IQ & conservative beliefs linked to prejudice. *LiveScience*. Retrieved from www.livescience.com/18132-intelligence-social-conservatism-racism.html.

19

ON HONESTY

WHAT'S BEST

It takes courage to be honest
It takes courage to be fair
It takes courage to remain authentic
When no one else seems to care

It takes grit to follow your passion
It takes guts to listen to your heart
It takes confidence to move in directions
That others consider less smart

It takes awareness to stay the course
It takes energy to find your zest
But why meekly go with the flow
When you already know what's best?

~ *Joan Marques*

Honesty is a virtue. And yet, it is not always easy to be honest. Sometimes the path of not telling the truth is the easier one out of a problem. Telling the truth could be the most courageous thing you will find yourself doing as a leader, especially when it infringes on policies, procedures, or opinions from those in positions of higher power than you.

In Buddhist psychology, honesty is described as "right speech" and as such, counts as one of the eight elements of the noble Eightfold Path, which is one of the most prominent behavioral vehicles within Buddhist practice. Whether we present honesty as truth telling or right speech: it entails a conscious effort to avoid lying, exaggerating, or downplaying things.

Unfortunately, some people have become so used to lying or shifting the truth in several ways, which they seem to have gotten completely out of touch with what Bill George would refer to as "Their True North" (their authentic self). Lying is harmful to the trust levels in relationships with others, but also with ourselves. Every lie we deliberately utter places a stain on our conscience that we will sooner or later have to deal with. This is something so many people overlook, especially when they are still young: their conscience. However, the conscience is the only thing no one else sees or feels. It's your own, and what you have placed there will be for you to deal with. The best favor you can do to yourself is to keep that conscience as clean as possible to omit future internal reckoning that can turn out to be so painful and devastating that it can lead to depression, long-term mental damage, or even worse.

A woman who has become known for her truth-telling courage is Binta Niambi Brown. She is currently the CEO and cofounder of Fermata Entertainment Ltd. She rose to prominence as a successful professional in law, human rights advocacy, media, and government, and then made a 190° shift in focus by establishing a music and entertainment business with a thus far unpracticed business model of focusing on maintaining the artists' rights and funding creative platforms that maximize personal expression and community connection. Her mission-oriented platform, B|G Mouth Records is vying to become the first statutory and certified B Corp.

Brown is a true octopus, as she finds her way through a brilliant career, yet, never loses sight of her humble beginnings. She sticks to her strongest believe, which is that honesty is the best strategy (Giang, 2015).

Early on in her career, Brown was confronted with the dilemma of telling the truth and potentially losing a lucrative contract, or keeping the truth hidden till the deal was sealed. She chose to practice right speech by telling the client of a $3 billion asset acquisition what she knew, thereby risking a major financial setback for herself and her business partner. She was well-aware that telling the truth at such a critical moment so early in her career could ruin the deal and be disastrous for her future professional path. She understood well that she was risking major reputation loss amongst colleagues. However, she decided that she could rather live with that than with concealing the truth to her client. Ultimately, the deal went through, and Brown learned an important lesson that paved the path of her business behavior from there on: honesty is the best strategy.

Another gem in the world of business leaders is Paul Polman, the now-retired CEO from Unilever, a global consumer product and food corporation, known for brands such as Lipton tea, Ben & Jerry's ice cream, and Vaseline skin care products. In early 2009, Paul Polman became the CEO of Unilever. The business world was still very much in the clutches of the global financial crisis, and Polman did what very few CEOs dare to do, especially new ones: he notified Unilever's shareholders that they should stop expecting quarterly and annual earnings guidance reports for the stock market. He stressed that the company was now going to take a longer view, and whoever was not happy about that could take their money and invest it somewhere else (Boynton, 2015).

Shortly after making this bold statement, Unilever's share price declined by 8%, because a fear emerged that there was bad news on the horizon in a company that had not done too well in recent history. But Polman, who was the first Unilever CEO in a long time to come in from the external environment rather than internally rising through the ranks (he previously worked at Procter & Gamble and Nestlé), did not stop there. He started disinviting some shareholders, which is quite unheard in business circles, and caused quite an upheaval in the company.

Polman, a major advocate for value creation and sustainable approaches, openly resented shareholders that are only out to get their money multiplied without really caring for the nature and behavior of the business they have invested it in. He affirmed that slavery had been abolished long ago, so shareholders should stop behaving as if they are slave drivers.

During his tenure at Unilever, Paul Polman saw his main responsibility to a large group of stakeholders, including consumers from all parts of the world and climate change activists. He took it as his leadership task to double Unilever's revenue while at the same time halving its environmental footprint. To that end, the company established the Unilever Sustainable Living Plan. While he understood that his ambitious goals would not be completely fulfilled during his tenure, he felt that he needed to initiate a change of mindset, which could then be carried on after him.

Polman didn't consider his vocal stance toward shareholders a demonstration of courage. He preferred to call it leadership, but asserted that courage enables you to put others' interests ahead of your own and be willing to take responsible risks. Polman was very much aware that a change toward massive adoption of a sustainable mindset would be a herculean task that would not happen overnight. He was aware that there would be many opponents and skeptics that would try to impede any effort toward doing the right thing in business. And indeed, he experienced opposition from companies that benefitted from keeping things as they were, such as the carbon-based industry. Yet, he considered every opposition an opportunity for future collaboration.

Paul Polman, who announced in November 2018 that he would step down as the chief executive officer of Unilever, particularly criticized Milton Friedman's teachings about the purpose of business to be self-serving and make profit, and do so without any further regard for the environment. He has always been an advocate for longer term thinking and continues to maintain a solid realization that business has a supporting function in the global economy, a need which he felt manifested itself clearly in the 2008 global financial crisis. Polman continues to believe in serving: in helping those that cannot help themselves. Among the many issues the world struggles with today are inequality, poverty, youth unemployment, and climate change, Polman believes that everyone—business included—should play a role in addressing them. So, aside from tending to environmental concerns, he focused Unilever's operations on livelihoods and social compliance. He was concerned about the large numbers of young people who are unemployed or hold marginal jobs in the world. He increased Unilever's sustainable sourcing from 10% in 2009, to 60%, but admitted during his leadership tenure that the company still has a long way to go.

In order to expand the circle of awareness, Polman engaged in a lot of networks, many of them consisting of young people and social entrepreneurs. This is how he encountered creative ideas and positive engagement, as well as hope that the world is getting closer to an overall awareness that we have to change our thought patterns toward more sustainable living. Polman also serves as Chairman of the World Business Council for Sustainable Development, member of the International Business Council of the World Economic Forum, member of the B Team and serves on the Board of the UN Global Compact and the Consumer Goods Forum, where he cochairs the Sustainability Committee.

Polman's efforts have been noticed by attentive and sustainability conscious sources. In 2017, he was recognized as one of the inaugural "Heroes of Conscious Capitalism" at the annual CEO Summit along with 27 other business leaders (Shawbel, 2017). He was recognized for his contribution toward realizing a world in which business is both practiced and recognized as a force for good.

As you may have discovered from the stories of Binta Niambi Brown and Paul Polman: they have discovered that honesty requires a lot of courage and can be a risky place to be, but it pays off in the end. Both of these leaders have found gratification in their career based on the reputation they build for themselves regarding their quality of truth telling.

References

Boynton, A. (July 20, 2015). Unilever's Paul Polman: CEOs can't be 'slaves' to shareholders. *Forbes*. Retrieved from www.forbes.com/sites/andyboynton/2015/07/20/ unilevers-paul-polman-ceos-cant-be-slaves-to-shareholders/#53da9874561e.

Giang, V. (June 6, 2015). 7 Business leaders share how they solved the biggest moral dilemmas of their careers. *Fastcompany.com*. Retrieved from www.fastcompany.com/30466 30/lessons-learned/7-business-leaders-share-how-they-solved-the-biggest-moral-dilemmas-of-their.

Shawbel, D. (November 1, 2017). Unilever's Paul Polman: Why today's leaders need to commit to a purpose. *Forbes*. Retrieved from www.forbes.com/sites/danschawbel/2017/11/21/ paul-polman-why-todays-leaders-need-to-commit-to-a-purpose/#32fb65411276.

20

ABOUT RESPECT

I recently saw a quote that stated, "You will never regret showing respect." Right beneath the quote, there were some interesting responses. One responder felt that you can get punished for being "too respectful," and another underscored this by reflecting on an incident at work, which she allotted to misplaced respect on her end.

I believe that we could all come up with examples of respect that was not properly acknowledged in our perception. You have probably also heard of the statement "No good deed goes unpunished." It is easy to attribute any disappointment that comes from interaction with another living being as abused respect.

Yet, I think the problem lies in the expectation we have regarding the respect we grant: this is what causes more disappointment than anything else. All too often, we expect reciprocity from the one to whom we have been respectful. In other words, if I have shown you respect, then you should return the favor. And while that would be nice, of course, there is just as little guarantee for that to happen, as there is in the promise that we'll see another day.

What we often forget to consider is the following:

Respect is an act onto itself. It should be like a second nature: deliberate, but not calculative, so it should not be tied to expectations.

The reward for our respect comes from unexpected places, at unexpected times, and in unexpected forms. When we least expect it, we will receive some kind of blessing.

It is interesting, however, that few of us wonder, when we are on the receiving end of life's generosities, what we did to deserve those. We just accept them and, if we're religious, we thank the lord or existence, but then we move on.

A more rational way of considering respect, and any other form of kindness for that matter, is as a humane duty: an unwritten rule for valuable and gratifying existence. The gratification starts when we stop expecting being respected in return from those to whom we have shown this form of courtesy. There is no misplaced respect. Any living being deserves it, for being part of this challenging earth and keeping themselves afloat.

There is a broader scope we should consider when thinking about respect: wherever we can lend extend it even further by lending a helping hand, we should give it. It is common courtesy, and yet, so hard to come across on a regular basis anymore. We are all so busy with getting ahead. Nothing wrong with that, as long as we keep in mind that, wherever we can, we should be respectful and kindhearted—without expectations—and refrain from harming others, and that doesn't only pertain to human beings.

This brings to mind a Zen story about two monks and a scorpion. The two monks were walking in the rain and saw a scorpion almost drowning in a water bowl. One of the monks reached into the bowl to save the scorpion, but it painfully stung him every time he tried. After witnessing this several times, the other monk asked his friend why he kept trying to save the stinging creature. As he finally picked up a leaf and released the scorpion that way, the monk smilingly said, "To sting is the scorpion's nature. To save is mine. My kindness and compassion are not discouraged that easily" (http://buddhistreflections.blogspot.com/2011/01/monk-and-scorpion.html).

Whether in professional, social, or private environments, we will encounter both, reciprocated and negligent responses to our respect and other forms of kindness. The best way to deal with any of these circumstances is to understand that no one owes us anything and that we will receive our share of respect and kindness in the right place, from the right source, and at the right time. No sooner, no later.

21

REGARDING SIMPLICITY AND HUMILITY

ONE MOMENT

In this one-moment breathe
I write a one-moment poem
To share some one-moment lines
With you

About this one-moment life that,
After one-moment struggles
And a one-moment glory,
Is through

We make one-moment fuss
Of a one-moment loss
And feel one-moment pride
For a one-moment stride

But this one-moment came
And the moment will go
And tomorrow we're all . . .
Well, you know . . .

~ Joan Marques

One of the interesting things to follow is the change in people's attitude as they grow. At first, as a child, we're helpless and, hence, dependent; then, with the decrease of our dependence, comes the increase of our self-confidence: we reach adolescence and we think we're immortal and indestructible; we grow into young adulthood with a conviction that the world will be at our feet because we are so special; and after that, gradually, we start to understand that we are not independent, but interdependent. That is when we realize that we are not only relying on our fellow human beings but also on our pets, plants, home, books, music, the weather, and many other things, in order to feel content. Every setback, disappointment, rejection, or wake-up call contributes to our growing sense of awareness that humility and simplicity are the most logical ways of existing.

Simplicity has nothing to do with simple-mindedness. On the contrary! If you manage to acknowledge the beauty of being simple, it indicates that you have reached a stage of wisdom that rises beyond every silly display of control and power. It also indicates that you figured out that real power lies within, and that business, home, or social activities are best practiced with a simple approach. Being simple is the strength that distinguishes the most admired business, political and religious leaders from the mediocre ones. To name and consider a few, Abraham Lincoln, Mohandas Gandhi, Nelson Mandela, Eva Duarte (Evita) Peron, Martin Luther King, Lady Diana, and, in the business section, Paul Pollman, Unilever's now-retired CEO, and Ray Anderson, founder and past CEO of Interface, one of the largest carpet tile factories. These strong people have all demonstrated that simplicity of character is not a determinant of intellect.

So, what we could conclude here, then, is that being simple and humble can best be associated with a state of being mature. Nevertheless, it is surely not the case that all older people are mature—as little as it is a fact that all younger people are immature. But it is a fact that the realization of the power of being simple and humble lies in having reached a stage of maturity, no matter your age. So what defines simplicity and humility? It might be better to first state what does not define them:

- Finances: Being simple and humble has nothing to do with the size of your bank account.
- Status: Being simple and humble is not reflected by your position at work. It has nothing to do with who you are part of the time, but more with how you are all of the time.
- Possessions: Being simple and humble is not mirrored by the car you drive or the house you live in. Locations and looks may be nice and desirable, but they don't ultimately define the level of your mental and emotional well-being.
- Your companions: Being simple and humble is not detectable through the people you interact with. Although you will choose your friends depending

on what you desire from life, especially when you realize that there is a difference between friends and acquaintances, they will not determine how you feel.

So, what defines being simple and humble, then?

Being simple and humble, in this perspective, is the sensation of oneness with everything and everyone around you. It can be identified as the realization that no one is really above or below you, no matter his or her position, status, or financial strength. This realization results in having respect for everyone: the rich and the poor, known and unknown, human and nonhuman. It can also be described as the realization that it is not foolish to grasp a hand that is being reached out to you, as little as it is foolish to reach out and have your hand grasped when necessary.

Being simple and humble brings about a feeling of contentment, even in times when your financial situation does not resemble the picture you had painted in your mind 20 years ago. Being simple and humble is seeing the beauty and greatness in everything, and being thankful for it. It's a matter of taking the time to smell the roses. And it is about realizing that life is too short to hold grudges, and too long—for the same reason.

Studying the topic of simplicity, Stuberg (1999) informed us that we should stop underestimating the power of simplicity. Many of us unnecessarily complicate our lives and fail to distinguish between the important and the futile issues. We tend to focus on activities instead of results. And as the pace of life continues to race along in the outside world, we forget that we also have the power to control our lives regardless of what's going on outside.

Zakrzewski (2016) wrote a wonderful essay on humility and explained therein that people who are truly humble set us at ease, which is a tremendous gift in today's rat race. The reason why humble people can do this is because they see and accept their own strengths and limitations without defensiveness or judgment. This, states Zakrzewski, is a core dimension, according to researchers, of humility, and one that cultivates a powerful compassion for humanity.

Indeed: the relief that taking it easy and untangling ourselves from the fuzziness of daily life is tremendous! Once you have mastered simplicity, peace of mind will be easy to achieve. Sleepless nights may not be total history, but the number of reasons for sleepless nights will be dramatically reduced. You may even start to get amused by perceiving all those who are striving for silly honors, while they come to you much easier, simply because you don't hustle them. Most of all, being simple and humble harbors the power of enlarging your horizon—understanding others better by giving them more attention, perceiving things more intensely, persevering for the right reasons with more dedication, listening to your intuition with more empathy, and still managing to bring the ones surrounding you in awe with your attitude. For being simple means, having the right and most admirable of all attitudes: the attitude of empathy.

Below are some points to ponder, with the aim to take a deeper look at areas where you might want to bring about changes toward living a life of greater simplicity and humility:

- Everything is about perception. We all have a tendency to look at things and situations we're confronted with from a most favorable (to us) point of view. However, if you stay in a (dreadful) situation out of fear for change in your current pattern, you're not being brave, but foolish: you're either fooling the rest of the world or yourself. And the latter is unforgivable!

- Every decision you make has an equal chance of turning out right or wrong, no matter how well prepared and thoroughly informed you are. It's what you do after you've made the decision that will determine the final outcome.

- No matter how hard it is to digest, failure is sometimes necessary for growth. Making a wrong decision; taking the wrong path may ultimately be a lesson you have to learn to become a wiser person.

- Everything you do eventually comes back to you. This is not a religion or culture-related philosophy: just plain truth. Therefore, doing well should not be seen as a luxury but as a self-preserving must!

- Everyone—even the most admired role models among us—has sometime, somehow, somewhere done something he or she is not too proud of. The passing of time and the consequential process of oblivion are therefore a blessing.

- The only person who knows the real motives behind your actions is you. Don't fool yourself.

- Every person you meet in whatever setting has an interesting story to tell. You may never get to know their story, but you can show the people you meet your respect anyway. They deserve it!

- Judging other people or cultures is easy to do from a personal or national perspective. Yet, realizing that you only have a limited view from where you stand; that you therefore don't have all the answers, and that you could have been part of that other group if nature had done its work slightly different, may create some empathy and understanding from your side.

- There are more unhappy people in the world than there are happy ones. Unhappiness is the discrepancy between what you can get, and what you really want. The easiest solution would be to adjust what you want to what you can get. Yet, also keep in mind that too much water dilutes the wine. Unhappiness may therefore just be a necessary part of most people's life: like a required shoe with a bad fit.

- Every positive attribute has a negative side to it depending on who analyses it and from what position. Determination can be seen as stubbornness; persuasiveness as pushiness, eloquence as blarney, different as ridiculous. The art is to keep a positive mindset, even if it's not propitious to you. The least you can do is to learn from it.

• No matter what your social standing, ethnic, educational, or cultural background is, we all have at least these two things in common: being born and dying. This, then, is the critical confirmation of the interconnectedness of all living creatures, for all plants, animals, and human beings share this very destiny. Shouldn't we therefore take good note of the things of every day; stop ridiculing ourselves by hiding behind our status, and show our real faces to each other on our journey from birth to death?

• Humility is no crime or shame: as long as you can feel content and satisfied with the way you earn your daily bread you're okay. And if you show compassion to others along the way, you will generate more from your work—financially and emotionally—than you initially expect. For goodness seldom goes unrecognized.

• Goals are great, but the way toward your goals should be worthwhile. Most of our lifetime we spend on our way toward goals anyway.

• Everything you do should be in line with your deepest conviction. If you take a step back and analyze what you're doing, it should all discharge into the one principle you strongly believe in. If that's not the case, you should consider where, how, and why you went astray.

• Your mindset radiates through your appearance. If you feel great and optimistic, you will shine and convince anyone of anything. But if you feel shattered and downtrodden, you may as well sleep the day away, for all efforts will be worth nothing.

• You only have one perspective: your own. However, your perspective can change through the books you read, the people you meet, the things you need, and life's general heat. Just as much as you can determine your attitude toward everything, you can also determine your perspective. Your biggest blunder would be to know that, yet refrain from doing it.

The contemplations listed earlier are, as you may have realized, applicable to all areas of our lives: work, home, or other settings. They can help adjust your perspectives, or at least, encourage you to consider the virtues of simplicity and humility. Consider them, and add your own life's findings to your version of the list. Then, proceed and make the best of the remainder of your journey. Good luck!

References

Einstein, A. (1999). TPCN—great quotations (Quotes) by Albert Einstein. Cyber Nation International, Inc. Retrieved April 28, 2002, from www.cyber-nation.com/victory/ quotations/authors/quotes_einstein_albert.html.

Sampter, J. (1999). TPCN—great quotations (Quotes) by Jessie Sampter. Cyber Nation International, Inc. Retrieved April 28, 2002, from www.cyber-nation.com/victory/ quotations/authors/quotes_sampter_jessie.html.

Stuberg, R. (1999). TPCN—great quotations (Quotes) by Stuberg. Cyber Nation International, Inc. Retrieved April 28, 2002, from www.cyber-nation.com/victory/quotations/authors/quotes_stuberg_robert.html.

Zakrzewski, V. (January 12, 2016). How humility will make you the greatest person ever: It's so hard to be humble. Here are three tips for taming your ego. *Greater Good Magazine*. Retrieved from https://greatergood.berkeley.edu/article/item/humility_will_make_you_greatest_person_ever.

22

ON ADAPTABILITY

The value of adaptability as a trait becomes apparent if we consider that everything we do could be seen as a game. People who have trained themselves to be flexible usually deal with less stress due to the fact that they are capable of releasing an impossible goal, and adjust their focus to a more realistic purpose.

The COVID-19 global pandemic that held the world in a paralyzing grip for a large part of 2020 moving into 2021, confronted humanity with the essence of being adaptable. Reality, as it had been customary before COVID-19 was wiped away and new modes of operation had to be invented and developed instantly. The term "unprecedented" became the new buzz term of the year, and its meaning manifested itself in practically every aspect of life: the divisive line between home and work blurred, and new ways of survival had to be formulated, along with new parameters of performance.

If we expand our perspective on the subject somewhat and generally perceive the significance of adaptability for all living species, we find that the types of animals and plants that have managed to survive through centuries are the ones that adapted to changed conditions. It is therefore definitely not an overstatement when we say that adaptability is the mental key to survival.

Professionally considered, adaptability can be the determining factor in keeping food on the table, be it that at some times the meals may be scantier than at others. But people who manage to pull themselves together after a job layoff, a relational breakup, or an unexpected but mandatory change of environment, will be able to find a renewed purpose in a relatively short time period because they have trained themselves to be adaptable.

Under the conspicuous title "Making change work for you—or at least not against you," McConnell (2002) states, "We can no longer find security in constancy, maintaining loyalty to the same ideas, concepts, and institutions for life. Rather, security, if such truly exists today, is more likely found in flexibility and adaptability" (pp. 66–77). Interesting point of view, isn't it?

McConnell then emphasizes an important aspect of adaptability by asserting:

> Flexibility and adaptability also equate with a degree of security when multiple skills reside in the same individual. The person who has taken every opportunity to learn and grow, to acquire new and different knowledge and skills, to become as versatile as possible, or who has actually become competent in two or three different occupational fields, stands a better chance of remaining employed-or securing new employment than the person who has remained limited to a single, narrow skill set.
>
> *(pp. 66–77)*

Adaptable people demonstrate resilience and are usually pleasant to work with. They can get used to any work situation, and blend themselves easily into any crowd. Although they may have one certain area of specialty or preference, they will start with whatever is offered to them, and inventively make their way to the place or position where they really want to be. Here's where strategy comes into play. What the adaptable individual does under such circumstances is to develop a plan through which he or she will get from the current position to the one desired. And even if it takes a few years and a number of initiatives that may be hard to understand by the rest of the world, he or she will get there. After all, an adaptable person is very often also a determined one. The first determination lies in not getting floored by any situation. The second one can be found in his or her willpower to succeed in whatever he or she starts!

In an almost two-decade-old article about the adaptability among Human Resource professionals, the outcomes of an annual survey from a New York consulting firm showed that "a significant number of HR professionals changing jobs were able to move into sales and marketing positions and that 11 of the 537 HR respondents reported that they had moved up to become CEO of their organization" (Bates, 2002, p. 23). Accentuating the importance of adaptability the article further states that "HR professionals are realizing that broader experience can really strengthen their career portfolio," and that "HR people are in a particularly good position to resell their competencies to different industries or different parts of an organization."

Rabkin and Bradford (2002) explain that organizations should realize that in our ever-changing world there are but two choices, "Adapt or Perish" (p. 45).

Although actually projected on the insurance market, the five keys that these authors present are useful as a self-examination tool toward everyone's capability on the way to adaptation. Here is a generalized version of the five keys:

1. Be aware of the environment. Register and rapidly process every new impulse.
2. Develop mechanisms for coping with discontinuous change: be quick and effective in responding to threats, regulations, expectations, or entirely different circumstances.

3. Experiment! Get acquainted with failure. And get acquainted with successful outcomes from others in the environment.
4. Innovate! Find new ways to do old things, and be prepared to do new things as well.
5. Keep yourself open for learning and—as a result to that—for reinventing yourself over and over again.

These rules may be the crucial ones for all living organisms that managed to survive, whether they were aware of applying them or not. This notion has been corroborated as recently as 2020 by Forbes' Business Council, where it is asserted that business leaders are well-aware of the importance of adaptability toward surviving market fluctuations and overcoming operational challenges successfully. Only when a person—or an organization—is able to pivot through unforeseen circumstances, will they be able to find solutions to problems.

So, adapt! Be Flexible! Diverge your capacities, for wallowing in bygone realities is a sure shot to failure.

References

Bates, S. (2002). HR professionals' adaptability shows up in the moves they make. *HRMagazine, 47*(10), p. 23.

Forbes Business Council. (June 11, 2020). Promoting a culture of adaptability: 16 effective tips for businesses. *Forbes—Small Business.* Retrieved from www.forbes.com/sites/forbesbusinesscouncil/2020/06/11/promoting-a-culture-of-adaptability-16-effective-tips-for-businesses/#5acb6d9a7139.

McConnell, C. (2002). Making change work for you—or at least not against you. *The Health Care Manager, 20*(4), pp. 66–77.

Rabkin, B., & Bradford, D. (2002). Evolution theory. *Best's Review, 103*(4), pp. 43–45.

23

ON NURTURING AN INNOVATIVE MINDSET

OUR OWN MAGICAL WAY

The human mind is powerful
And yet, so vulnerable and frail
Today we may burst with creativity
Tomorrow our thoughts may be stale

Our circumstances often dictate
The quality of what we produce
Optimism leads to uplifting thoughts
While setbacks can serve as a noose

Yet, there's blessing in every mood
As life's lessons arise every day
And reflecting upon them is key
To help us pave our own magical way

~ Joan Marques

Inspiration is one of the cornerstones of making progress. We all get inspired by different things at different times, but how many of us take the time to actually consider where our inspiration comes from? One thing is sure: Inspiration does not allow itself to be forced, not onto ourselves, and definitely not onto others. When I was asked to present a talk on where I have found inspiration in my life,

I came up with five sources, which, as I learned afterward, are fairly identifiable for most people. These sources are also powerful foundations toward acquiring and nurturing an innovative mindset. They are as follows.

Setbacks

When setbacks hit us, they don't feel inspiring at all. They don't even feel good. Yet, every setback has a lot to teach us, and we often find, much later, what the purpose was of having experienced the setback. Losing a job, going through a divorce, having to move out of a familiar environment, letting go of something or someone precious, failing to be selected for the job we aimed for, being diagnosed with an illness: The list of setbacks can be enormous. While the setback itself is never a great experience, it is usually the onset to a new stage in our life.

Setbacks trigger transformation, and transformation leads to change. A friend of mine experienced this when he went through his divorce. After 25 years of marriage, he had not anticipated ever having to start anew, but once breakup time was there, he knew that looking back would only lead to depression. So, he looked ahead and reinvent himself. He decided to focus on higher education and earned a Masters and a doctorate to reformat and innovate his life from that angle. Over the course of time, he met someone, got remarried, and settled in an entirely different type of life than he previously had. He now realizes the inspiration he gained from the distressing divorce experience, and how, in hindsight, it inspired him to build a new, rewarding life.

People

People can inspire us through positive and negative encounters. In positive situations, it may be their helpfulness or their caring attitude that inspires us: A way of reaching out to us that confirms that we are on the right track and that gives us a new boost of determination. The inspiration from negative encounters usually happens in retrospection, just as with setbacks. One of my colleagues likes to tell the story of a very unpleasant encounter she had with her supervisor in a previous job. The supervisor was disturbed by my colleague's ambition, which manifested itself in hard work and performance beyond the call of duty. At the first possible window for evaluation, the supervisor expressed her discontentment, and told my colleague that there was no place for both of them in the department. After consulting with her mentors, my colleague decided to resign from the job, and within six months acquired a position she had aspired all along. Had she stayed in the dreadful situation, there would have not been an opportunity for innovative actions. Today, my colleague is happy and satisfied with her career, and feels grateful about the boldness of this former supervisor, as this inspired her to let go of a job that might have been a reasonable choice, but not by far as great and fulfilling as the one she holds today.

Inner Connection

A valuable source of inspiration toward innovation is our inner core. We often ignore this source, because it is always there, and we have a tendency to overlook the things closest to us. In 2008, I traveled to Dharamsala, India, to interview a team of seasoned Tibetan Buddhist Monks for a study project. I used the opportunity to participate in a ten-day Vipassana meditation retreat and fell in love with this practice of insight meditation. What a treasure to have the ability of turning inward whenever and wherever we prefer to do so and observe our innermost sentiments about anything. A calm retreat to our inner world can help us find answers to problems we struggle with or provide us inspiration for new directions. It helps us see things in a different, more wholesome perspective, so that we can better understand what should be a priority in our life and whatnot.

Mindfulness practices can help us relieve much of our daily stress, because they enable us to "zoom out," look at the bigger picture, and dwell less on the waves of daily life with all their highs and lows and the emotional roller coaster they can cause. Increasing our inner connection can bring us more mental and emotional stability, and inspire us to step over the bumps that would otherwise irritate and discourage us toward new, innovative, and promising horizons.

Noble Acts

Life provides us many opportunities every day anew to engage in noble acts. Whether these selfless acts pertain to people, animals, or plants, they are equally inspiring. Noble acts are a form of giving without an agenda, and there is no pleasure as enduring as the pleasure of selfless giving. Yielding for someone in traffic, helping someone across the street, feeding the homeless neighborhood cat, or making a donation to a homeless person or a good cause: These are all sources of inspiration because they make us feel good about what we do, and when we feel good, we have a better chance of finding our inspiration, and see paths toward innovations we might have otherwise never encountered, let alone entertained.

Education

This source can be interpreted in two ways: Our own education and the education we provide to others. In regard to our own education, whether this is formal or informal, we owe it to ourselves to keep on learning. It is not necessarily what we learn, but the ability we develop from regular learning, that will benefit us in life overall. People who continuously educate themselves develop a greater ability to think more critically and creatively about everything. They, therefore, don't take anything as a given and conjure up new insights and ideas where others just accept the status quo.

In regard to educating others, this too can happen in formal and informal settings, but it is always a great reward when we find that those who once listened to our advice have found their place in life.

SPINE, the first letters of these five inspiration sources, means backbone. Inspiration, which leads to innovation, is the backbone of our performance.

24

ABOUT EMPATHY

Empathy can be defined as "the action of [or capacity for] understanding, being aware of, being sensitive to, and vicariously experiencing the feelings, thoughts, and experience of another of either the past or present without having the feelings, thoughts, and experience fully communicated in an objectively explicit manner" (Merriam-Webster, 2020). In simpler terms, "It's the ability to step outside of yourself and see the world as other people do" (Patnaik, 2009, p. 8).

A Professional View on Empathy

Although empathy is no longer considered merely a "soft" skill, but more and more a professional ability, it is hard to quantify. Just like how intricate it is to assign numeric value to a company's goodwill on its balanced scorecard, empathy, being intangible, is difficult to measure. Hence the scarcity of empirical studies on correlations between companies' efficiency and the role empathy plays in their organizational cultures. Nevertheless, such studies, which tie empathy to business results, are attempted more frequently, especially in studies of sales and product development, with terms like "empathy marketing" and "user empathy," becoming mainstream.

Indeed, in the increasingly immediate, intimate, world driven by rapid change, where everyone has to be proficient at identifying opportunities and solving problems, the case for empathy in business could not be stronger. Companies make money by designing, producing, and selling what customers need (or want). Without understanding what the customers want, there is no business. Without empathy, the capacity to put yourself in others' situations, and meet these others where they are, there is no understanding of the customers' needs. And retaining existing ones is far less expensive than securing new ones.

A similar logic can be applied to employees: happy employees are better than just employees, as profits are to a large extent a derivative of devoted staff. Consequently, businesses should be concerned with engagement of their personnel. At the time when many employees report lack of engagement, studies reveal that employee engagement promotes enhanced organizational outcomes, such as job performance and job satisfaction—which, in turn, lead to business growth and profitability. Research also shows that there is a positive relationship between good relations and employee engagement, as well as a direct relationship between shared vision and a positive work environment is essential in concentrating attention, stimulating interest, and moving people to act.

Companies do not do business with other companies. The people in these companies do business with each other. Successful people and companies do not operate in a vacuum. For organizations to be effective, they must be empathetic to resident differences, appreciate the emotional makeup of other people, and know-how to build and manage relationships and networks. Individuals need to communicate, work in teams, and let go of the issues that interfere with their performance. Interpersonal skills such as communication and relating to people from diverse backgrounds are indispensable qualities for success in our workplace.

Unfortunately, the focus on empathy and employee and customer satisfaction are often considered less important than short-term corporate results. What many business leaders overlook is that there is a positive relationship between emotional development and socioeconomic behavior (Ackert & Church, 2001; Elster, 1998; Keynes, 1964). So perhaps it would be safe to suggest that in today's interconnected economic system, supply and demand are not driven only by basic needs but also by emotional tendencies. Empathy may be part of the solution when incorporated in decision-making without compromising business judgment.

True empathy combines understanding of logical and emotional rationale and is the driving power behind effective communication.

Overall, personal attributes that are effective in nature are increasingly highlighted in the workplace, and studies show that emotional functioning capacities are linked to workplace readiness. In recent years especially, leadership effectiveness has been examined extensively in connection with emotional management as a critical factor for organizational success, with strong positive correlations found between managers' emotional management skills and employee motivation and productivity (Drager, 2014; Bartock, 2013; Park, 2013).

Businesses that do not espouse a bigger purpose than generating profit will have a hard time maintaining relationships with their investors, customers, and surrounding communities. Work environments that espouse empathy-based moral reasoning are more likely to be socially and economically successful. Being attuned to and empathetic toward stakeholders' needs helps businesses to formulate and hone their strategies.

A recent study on customer satisfaction and loyalty confirms a statistically significant relationship between empathy and customer loyalty (Lartey, 2015).

Especially in entrepreneurship, empathy is essential to sustainable achievement. From shareholders to investors, from customers to employees, entrepreneurs have to be able to tune into the needs and outlooks of all their stakeholders. Empathy allows them to create bonds of trust, and such connection, in turn, allows them to run their businesses best. It is essential, too, that stakeholders are confident that their interests are taken into account, and, consequently, entrepreneurs need to be able to empathize with their stakeholders' anxieties and perceptions.

Empathy implies an ability to understand and take active interest in others by recognizing changes in their emotional states through reading body language and verbal clues and being perspicuous about the underlying reasons of these changes. By matching appropriate behaviors to respective work environments, businesses stimulate followers' motivation, which, in turn, leads to greater organizational effectiveness. Therefore, modern enterprises are challenged with the task of enhancing the emotional management skills of their leaders, who must acquire and practice their empathy and social skills through self-learning as much as job-related training. Organizations may also need to refine their recruiting policies to focus on prospective leaders' emotional management skills to a greater extent than on their technical skills and experience (Lartey, 2015).

Empathy is a valuable commodity, and for those of us to whom it does not come naturally, there is good news—it can be cultivated. Martinuzzi (2009) compares it to a muscle which strengthens with repeated use. According to Cohen (2012), in their business ethics courses, schools should focus on nurturing empathetic practice instead of emphasizing moral reasoning as a tactic for creating mutually favorable outcomes. According to the author, the reason for unethical behavior is not poor ethical reasoning but the lack of understanding and care about what others feel because we have never had similar experiences. Taking a personal interest in others, practicing being fully present, listening, and tuning into nonverbal communication clues are paths to training our "empathy muscles" (Martinuzzi, 2009).

A Personal View on Empathy

Having the ability to understand others deeply is a great virtue, but it can lead to complexity in one's life as well.

Empathy is often portrayed as one of the outstanding skills an individual should have in order to be a good leader. And rightfully so: a leader who is capable of empathizing with his or her followers is usually seen as a transformational one because he or she knows how to make his or her subordinates feel that they matter not just as a segment in the workplace, but as a holistic being in various settings. An empathetic leader will be praised for his or her "sixth" sense, because this leader will invest every possible effort to make people feel happy in their job by placing them in positions they can handle well, and therefore, excel in.

But empathy is not just a virtue in work-related environments: an empathetic individual is usually dearly loved by many far outside the work setting. Empathetic people know how to make you feel that they care and that they are willing to do anything they can to make you happy and keep you content. And here is where the problem creeps in: They often do that at their own expense! A highly empathetic person may develop such a need to keep others happy that he or she totally ignores his or her own happiness. Why? Because he or she perceives his or her happiness as a selfish act, especially if others will be hurt on the way toward achieving it.

An example may be in place here: An empathetic person who is attached to a partner or team that desperately needs him or her may realize that his or her happiness lies somewhere else, and may even already have identified the location, setting, or person with whom happiness will be a fact, but for the mere reason that he or she knows the despair that will be caused by leaving the current partner or team, he or she discards his or her own chance of emotional comfort. Yes, empathetic people may therefore be called people pleasers. And yes, empathetic people may even be considered cowards. But is that really the case? I guess it depends on the angle you perceive it from: it is cowardice to fear the encounter with pain, but at the same time it is brave to stay where you don't really want to be.

There are many people who stay with partners, jobs, projects, or teams that they actually dread, simply because they dread the hurt they will cause by leaving even more. And again, it may not even be fear for change that is ruling here, as the empathetic person may very well be an adventurous one: it may just be plain old fear for causing pain. Arrogant? Maybe! For one never knows how resilient these "dependent" partners, jobs, projects, or teams may turn out to be once the empathetic person really dares to take the big step of leaving. But that may never happen, as empathetic people keep ciphering themselves away and keep prioritizing the needs of those who are actually the more successful ones: the ones that know how to express their needs in order to keep the empathetic soul paralyzed.

So, what can we learn from this? Perhaps the following: empathy is a virtue, but like any other virtue, it should be applied mindfully. Too much understanding and empathizing may lead to personal unhappiness for the sake of the well-being of others.

References

Ackert, L., & Church, B. (2001). The effects of subject pool and design experience on rationality in experimental asset markets. *Journal of Psychology and Financial Markets, 1*, pp. 6–28.

Bartock, A. L. (2013). Fight or flight, stay or leave: The relationship between emotional intelligence and voluntary turnover. (Order No. 3585950, University of Phoenix). ProQuest Dissertations and Theses, 312. Retrieved from http://search.proquest.com/docview/1512420679?accountid=13159 (1512420679).

Cohen, M. A. (2012). Empathy in business education. *Journal of Business Ethics Education*, *9*(1), p. 359.

Drager, K. A. (2014). Examining the ability of emotional intelligence and work location to predict job satisfaction. (Order No. 3611231, Capella University). ProQuest Dissertations and Theses, 124. Retrieved from http://search.proquest.com/docview/1502015688?accountid=13159 (1502015688).

Elster, J. (1998). Emotions and economic theory. *Journal of Economic Literature*, *36*, 47–74.

Keynes, J. M. (1964). *The General Theory of Employment, Interest, and Money*. First Harbinger Edition and Harvest/Harcourt Brace Jovanovich, New York, NY.

Lartey, F. M. (2015). Increasing promoters in the residential broadband service industry: Relationship between customer satisfaction and loyalty using ordinal logistic regression (Order No. 3682580). Available from ProQuest Dissertations & Theses Global; ProQuest Dissertations and Theses A&I: The Humanities and Social Sciences Collection. Retrieved from http://search.proquest.com/docview/1658144293?accountid=13159 (1658144293).

Martinuzzi, B. (2009). *The Leader as a Mensch: Become the Kind of Person Others Want to Follow*. Six Seconds, San Francisco, CA.

Merriam-Webster. (2020). Empathy. Retrieved from www.merriam-webster.com/dictionary/empathy.

Park, H. H. (2013). Determinants on mechanism of emotional marketing: Emotional intelligence, perception of emotional labor' action, efficacy and customer' coping strategy on customer satisfaction. (Order No. 3598952, Oklahoma State University). ProQuest Dissertations and Theses, 188. Retrieved from http://search.proquest.com/docview/1461742750?accountid=13159 (1461742750).

Patnaik, D. (2009). *Wired to Care: How Companies Prosper When They Create Widespread Empathy*. FT Press, New York, NY.

25

THOSE SOFT SKILLS OVERALL

Soft skills entail qualities such as motivation, empathy, self-awareness, self-regulation, and social skills (Goleman, 2000). A person who applies soft skills focuses on a combination of interpersonal and social skills (Dixon et al., 2010). At the other end of the spectrum are the "hard" or "tough" skills, which include drive, rigor, vision, intelligence, analytical and technical skills (Goleman, 2000). Most of the hard or tough skills can be measured and quantified. Based on the explanation mentioned previously, you may already surmise that both soft and hard skills are important in leading yourself and others, because they complement one another.

For the longest time, leadership was considered to be all about charisma, confidence, and superior knowledge. The sensitive characteristics were considered out of place in work environments. Unfortunately, there are still workplaces, corporate, entrepreneurial, and even academic, that have managers who think that the only way to supervise is through hard skills. Leaders, who have patted themselves on the back for years about their "no-nonsense" approach of intelligence, vision, and rational decision-making, still feel that soft skills should not have a place in the workplace, and resist any coaching in that regard, even though they really want to do a good job (Newell, 2002). The idea that empathy and its related behaviors should stay out of the work floor is just too deeply embedded in their system, even if they are told about the results that such a shift in behavior would bring, and learn about successful companies that included soft skills in their leadership strategies.

It is a fact, however, that soft skills come easier to some than to others. Particularly those leaders, who have been trained with a major left-brain orientation (accounting, finance, economics, mathematics, science, and engineering based), may find it difficult to tap into their right brain for some empathy and gentle motivation (Nyman, 2006). These leaders, who by default heavily rely on their intelligence and credentials, should be approached in a methodical way, and invited to scan their workplace and find out how others see them, so that they can consider making adjustments to their behavior. They need to gradually be introduced to the awareness that leading people requires a different type of intelligence than the one they internalized during their job specializations. These leaders, who have always been used to focus only on measurable information in their decision-making processes, and who have always been used to accuse others of anything that went wrong, now have to become familiarized with the idea that their intuition could be a useful guide, and that they need to expand their internal locus of control by accepting the blame when they are at fault (Gaillour, 2004).

Over the past two decades, several studies have been done on soft versus hard skills, with amazingly divergent outcomes. It seems that smaller work environments prefer a decent balance in soft and hard skills to nurture a constructive and engaging atmosphere, while large corporations still seem to adhere to hard skills, especially in top positions. Fortunately, the latter has changed in recent years, and even Ivy League schools such as Harvard Business School have engaged in more soft skills-based courses and studies.

Important to know for any leader is that soft skills create a trust relationship between employees and their leader, and when employees trust their leader, they will support him or her in easy and challenging times. Leaders who ignore the importance of building trust may find themselves isolated when they need those around them most. Trust has major impact on how others perceive us, and so does the lack of it. The excessive emphasis on hard skills in the recent past has led to major trust problems in workplaces: employees who believe that their managers only care for short term outcomes and not for their well-being will not trust this manager, and not share their honest opinions with him or her because they may be fearful that they will be penalized. Similarly, middle managers who believe that their supervisors only care for the bottom line will not trust them, and possibly withhold critical information from them, either for fear or spite. Of course, we should not forget the customers and other stakeholders, who are also aware of the reputation of the companies they deal with: if they are aware that they are dealing with a corporation that has leaders who are greedy, severely detached, and uncaring toward their lower level employees, they will not be very loyal to this corporation. What may become apparent here is that an overemphasis on hard skills damages trust in all layers of an organization's hierarchy, and all facets of its performance.

The very nature of today's work environment is ambiguous and requires adaptability, understanding, and great communication skills. This all underscores the lasting importance of soft skills in the world of work as we know it today, and as we will know it in the future.

References

Dixon, J., Belnap, C., Albrecht, C., & Lee, K. (2010). The importance of soft skills. *Corporate Finance Review, 14*(6), pp. 35–38.

Gaillour, F. R. (2004). Want to be CEO? Focus on finesse. *Physician Executive, 30*(4), pp. 14–16.

Goleman, D. (2000). Leadership that gets results. *Harvard Business Review, 78*(2), pp. 78–90.

Newell, D. (2002). The smarter they are the harder they fail. *Career Development International, 7*(5), pp. 288–291.

Nyman, M. (2006). Want to be a topflight leader? Hone your people skills. *Chemical Engineering, 113*(8), pp. 63–65.

26
OPENNESS TO DIVERSITY

CONFRONTING OUR BIASES

Where is the truth? That virtuous friend:
Impartial reality without a smudge?
It lives outside our biased mind
And is, regrettably, hard to find
In the mental rubble through which we judge

Our biases are alive and well
Fueling our views and emotions
Culture, religion, family and peers
They instilled in us the joys and fears
That now influence many of our notions

Being aware of this human shortfall
Is dreadful, but also enlightening
As it motivates our brains
To transcend their constraints
And embrace what once seemed frightening

It's been too long now, that we indulged
In thoughts of inferior versus supreme
Judging on accents, sex, skin-colors
Age, skills, or assumed wealth in dollars
It's time to release that obsolete dream

> Becoming mindful of our biases
> Is liberating and drives spiritual rebirth
> None of us stands beneath or above
> The ability to embrace and love
> All that lives with us on Mother Earth
>
> ~ *Joan Marques*

There are many definitions related to diversity, depending on the context in which it is used. In light of the topic at hand, diversity could be defined as a concept, which includes every way in which people can differ (Carrell et al., 2006). Diversity has earned more attention in the past few decades, as we experienced an increase in human interaction at a level that had not been possible before. This massive exposure has not only given rise to greater awareness but has also spawned a continuous quest from business leaders for inexpensive resources and lower labor costs. In societal as well as organizational settings, there is, additionally, an increasing need for diverse teams to address issues of ongoing complexity (Gotsis & Kortezi, 2013). These and other trends result in increasingly diversified workforces at local, regional, and international levels.

Diversity can be an advantage or a problem in any organization, depending on the way it is addressed and how intensely it is nurtured. A major factor therein is employees' perspectives of their treatment: when they feel that they have equal access to opportunities and that they are treated fairly, they will feel more satisfied, which causes the diversity implementation to become more successful, because the work progresses and turn over decreases (Chrobot-Mason & Aramovich, 2013).

Yet, there is no real definition for workplace diversity. The concepts for either diversity or diversity management are too complex to formulate an unambiguous definition (Meriläinen et al., 2009). This lack of a unified definition, especially for diversity management, could be because it is so dependent on the cultural dynamics of different societies and labor markets (Tatli & Özbilgin, 2009). Although a clear definition is risky to formulate, workplace diversity includes, among others, people from various ethnicities, genders, responsibilities, cultural backgrounds and statuses, sexual preferences, abilities, and age groups (Harvey & Allard, 2008).

As matters currently stand, however, corporations are quick to claim on their corporate websites that they apply diversity, and technically, this claim could not be denied. Yet, the application of workplace diversity does not always happen for the right reasons. When we consider the reasons why corporations—and their leaders—implement diversity, we could produce a long list, varying from very proactive to very reactive. Let's now consider four insufficient, yet frequently occurring corporate reasons for implementing diversity.

Customer-Based Diversity

This is when leaders assemble a workforce that reflects their customer base. While this is commendable, it should not be the only driving motive for having a diverse workforce, as its purpose is solely bottom-line driven. Leaders in these organizations are not necessarily convinced that diversity is the morally proper thing to do. The only point of concern to them is that their customers feel at ease in the store by recognizing salespeople who resemble them.

When we examine these corporations more closely, we detect that their diversity trend resides at the lower levels where workers meet customers. The controlling mechanisms often remain with a homogeneous group. Unfortunately, homogeneous groups lack the comprehensive depth of diverse teams in decision-making, so they unintentionally obstruct the organization from valuable growth opportunities.

Single-Minded Diversity

In single-minded diversity, leaders base their diversity efforts on a unifying ideology, often centered on a single-minded religious, philosophical, or legal motive, to which all employees are expected to adhere. While such initiatives lead to physical manifestations of diversity, it discourages perceptional diversity, which is where the real value of this phenomenon lies.

Moreover, single-minded diversity can inhibit employees that don't adhere to the mindset of the leaders and end in greater turnover. This results in declining profits, because companies with large turnover have to continuously hire and train new employees, which are time and money consuming, and reflects poorly on customer groups who continuously encounter new company representatives.

Trend-Based Diversity

In trend-based diversity, organizational leaders are aware that diversity is a critical trend today. They may have read about it, or witnessed competitors successfully implementing it, so they do it, yet fail to prepare a proper foundation. In some of these instances, top management mainly gives orders to create a diverse workforce, but further remains uninvolved in the complications of dealing with the workforce. This disconnect may lead to regress instead of progress in the organization's performance because employees soon sense the lack of support for their divergent perspectives and alternative ideas. As described in single-minded diversity mentioned previously, the lack of support and recognition will lead to larger turnover and end up costing the company precious time and money to rehire and retrain new employees. This cost- and time ineffective process may serve as a welcome justification to a diversity-averse top-management team to demonstrate that the diversity efforts did not pay off in their corporation. Based on this evidence, the homogeneous, group-think trend can ultimately be restored.

Locally Accommodating Diversity

In locally accommodating diversity, leaders attract employees to serve local demographics in the areas where their organization has performance units, but fail to allow employees to learn from one another or move up through the ranks. In other words, such corporations diversify geographically, thus hiring employees that are deemed "appropriate" on the basis of locally perceived needs. For instance, black employees are hired for the predominantly black areas of operations, gay–lesbian–bisexual–transgendered (GLBT) employees for regions that are known to be progressive in that regard, and older workers are attracted in areas where the population is primarily conservative. The diversity in these types of corporations is solely implemented for local accommodation, thus leading to glass ceilings for some groups of employees. The main concern with this reason for implementing diversity is that everyone tends to stay in his or her corner, and opportunities to learn from one another are limited. Consequently, the deeper advantages of diversity—mutual learning, mindset expansion, greater acceptance, and enhanced insights—remain uncultivated.

Diversity as It Should Be Implemented

Proper implementation of a diversity initiative first and foremost requires the involvement of leaders. The reasons for engaging in diversity, the short- and long-term consequences for the organization and its stakeholders, and the procedures to follow should be seriously considered, and employees of various backgrounds, religions, age groups, sexes, and other distinctions should be properly guided in the process of acceptance. It should also be understood that conflict is inevitable where different worlds meet, because human beings have an innate tendency to think their way is better than others. It takes time and tact to change people's perceptions in this regard. Yet, once this occurs, the process of intermingling and bringing to the table the best options of multiple worlds can lead to rewarding outcomes for the organization and all individuals involved. Overall performance improves, and each worker experiences the personal gratification of horizon expansion (Marques, 2007).

Why We Should Embrace Diversity

As a general note, here are seven critical reasons to consider in the process of embracing workplace diversity:

1. In light of ethical leadership, it is just the right thing to do, and leaders should keep track of a proper representation of diversity in their workforce, from bottom levels to top levels.
2. It is an important support mechanism in compliance with diversity and anti-discrimination laws.

3. A company with a diverse workforce has better marketing opportunities, based on the fact that multiple customer groups can identify with the company's workforce.
4. A diverse workforce produces better and more widely considered outcomes, thus guaranteeing more creativity and an increased competitive advantage.
5. Potential employees from a wide range of backgrounds will acquire the desire to work for a diverse company, because it is easy for them to identify with the workforce.
6. Diversity can be a powerful retainer for employees, as they can tell that they are valued as persons in their own right, regardless of whom or what they represent.
7. Diversity may positively impact the bottom line, because satisfied employees are more willing to elevate their workplace to a higher performance plane (*Turning Diversity . . .*, 2007).

References

Carrell, M. R., Mann, E. E., & Sigler, T. H. (2006). Defining workforce diversity programs and practices in organizations: A longitudinal study. *Labor Law Journal, 57*(1), pp. 5–12.

Chrobot-Mason, D., & Aramovich, N. P. (2013). The psychological benefits of creating an affirming climate for workplace diversity. *Group & Organization Management, 38*(6), pp. 659–689.

Espinoza, M. (2007). Turning diversity into a competitive advantage. *Financial Executive, 23*(3), pp. 43–46.

Gotsis, G., & Kortezi, Z. (2013). Ethical paradigms as potential foundations of diversity management initiatives in business organizations. *Journal of Organizational Change Management, 26*(6), pp. 948–976.

Harvey, C. P., & Allard, M. J. (Eds.). (2008). *Understanding and Managing Diversity* (4th ed.). Pearson Prentice Hall, Upper Saddle River, NJ.

Marques, J. F. (2007). Implementing workplace diversity and values: What it means, what it brings. *Performance Improvement, 46*(9), pp. 5–7.

Meriläinen, S., Tienari, J., Katila, S., & Benschop, Y. (2009). Diversity management versus gender equality: The Finnish case. *Canadian Journal of Administrative Sciences, 26*(3), pp. 230–243.

Tatli, A., & Özbilgin, M. F. (2009). Understanding diversity managers' role in organizational change: Towards a conceptual framework. *Canadian Journal of Administrative Sciences, 26*(3), pp. 244–258.

27
WHAT'S UP WITH REFLECTION

AVOID FUTURE PAIN

Feeble, fickle, and frail
Is the path we tread
When we seek our passion
In earning our daily bread

Finding meaning and purpose
While generating our monthly pay
Considering the effects of our actions
In a future—far beyond today

There's so much to reflect on
In defining a truly rewarding mission
What, how, who, where, and when . . .
Never wavering from our future's vision

There's infinitely more fulfillment
In honest and awakened gain
In remaining kind and mindful
And avoiding any future pain . . .

~ Joan Marques

It is impossible to go through life without feelings and thoughts. These feelings and thoughts affect your body and your mind and can bring you in various mental states, from elation to devastation.

However, as you mature, you also learn that nothing lasts: not elation, not devastation, and not anything in between. Feelings and thoughts come and go like the tides of a river. If your responses to emotions are like those of the majority of other human beings, you probably enjoy the feelings of elation and dread those of devastation. You may then have also learned that elation, devastation, and all in-between states can elicit behaviors in you that you would have avoided, were you in a more moderate state of mind.

Fortunately, there is a way to establish a better balance in your life, in which neither elation nor devastation, nor any state in between, will derail your acts or your perspectives about what makes sense, and whatnot. That is the way of observation.

By observing your states mindfully, you learn to see them in their right perspectives. You also learn to see their origins, so you get to understand them better and consequently release them from additional baggage that merely engorges their volume and, thus, blows them out of proportion. It is, after all, this blowing out of proportion, which creates extremes such as elation and devastation.

This is not to say that mindful analysis of your feelings and thoughts will entirely eliminate extreme emotional experiences, as you are still part of this world, and there will still be events that will bring out intense emotions within you at times, due to your connectedness with other living beings. However, it does entail that there will be fewer outliers and more balance in your states from then on.

So how do you observe yourself?

1. Examine your emotions and thoughts from an outsider's perspective whenever you think about them (for instance: "Boy, am I upset today!").
2. Realize what exactly it is that you are feeling or thinking now ("I experience a feeling of disappointment").
3. Analyze how this feeling or thought came about ("I experience a feeling of disappointment because my colleague at work whom I considered a friend told others something I had shared confidentially with him or her").

Once you have detected the nature of your feeling or thought (2) and its reason for existence (3), you can start working at it: in the example given earlier you can either decide not to trust this colleague anymore, or you can express your disappointment about his or her actions.

In either of the steps you decide to take in order to balance this emotion, you have to make sure it frees you from the excessive sentiment, and transforms this feeling into one that you can easier accept. Yet, it may also be wise not to forget the lesson you learned from this feeling or emotion, which, in this case, may be to remain friendly and kind, but to refrain from, or be more careful about, sharing confidential information with others in the future.

One thing you should definitely refrain from is becoming and remaining upset at yourself. You are the one closest to your feelings and thoughts, so you better keep them bearable toward yourself.

By engaging in observation about your mental and emotional states, you will get better insight into your character: your strengths, weaknesses, likes, dislikes, interests, and noninterests. It is this evaluation of your feelings and thoughts and their origins that will ultimately eliminate most extremes and make you a better balanced person, more capable of coping with the surprises of life, overall.

28

CONSIDERING SUCCESS

NOTHING NEW

We're born with 'possessing' as our aim
Because we were given a bodily frame
Which we've come to cherish and adore
As if that's who we are, and nothing more
So, our life becomes an enduring stride
Of chasing possessions, people, and pride
We accumulate anything to make us feel
That the 'physical self' illusion is real
And most of us are devoted to this trend
Until the day comes that it all has to end
The day that we have to give up the stride
Thus, all the possessions, people, and pride
And then we have to surrender the body too
It's an old, recurring story. Nothing new.

~ *Joan Marques*

Success has numerous definitions, but in the end, you are the only one to define what it means to you. In fact, the answer to the question "what is success?" could be regarded as simple as $1 + 1 = 2$: Everything that makes you feel good! And yet, there is so much more depth to this answer than the seeming logic of it, just as there is in the simple equation mentioned previously. You know that $1 + 1$ is only 2 in abstract mathematics, right? In every other aspect it can just as easily be zero as it can be three . . . or more. The secret behind the level of outcome? Simple! The rate of success in the combination of the components, in this case: the two ones.

Think of the law of real estate: if you have one nice piece of property in a classy neighborhood, it may represent a decent value. However, if you manage to purchase an adjacent piece of land, your property will suddenly be worth more than the sum of both separate pieces, because you now own a far more accommodating, convenient, and desirable plot of land there!

Another catchy example of the 1 + 1 dilemma: couples! Ever seen two people teaming up and not achieving any degree of happiness, success, or fortune, while another couple with similar backgrounds, yet a different combination of characteristics, manages to stick together, build an empire of millions, beget and raise five happy kids, and renew their honeymoon every year with a breathtaking cruise through the Caribbean? In the first case, 1 + 1 ended in zero—and in the second, the sky was the limit!

So, what exactly constitutes success?

1. Chemistry: between you and whatever you want to achieve. If it makes you happy and you manage to achieve it, you're a winner, even if no one else cares.
2. Ability: this may vary from one goal to another. Sometimes you will need emotional ability to win, and at other times it may be financial power, brain sharpness, or persuasive skills. The key is to know when to apply which ability (or set of abilities), to what degree, and in which particular blend.
3. Intuition: as just mentioned: knowing which abilities to apply, when, and in which combinations, requires a sensitivity that only intuition can provide. Besides: you will also need intuition to determine whether to go for that particular goal at all! And if so, whether this is the time to do so!
4. Mindset: stay focused. Once distracted, you may lose sight—and grip—of your goal.
5. Humor: you must definitely be able to laugh off the slips and slides you will certainly make on your way to becoming a winner.
6. Creativity: no matter how focused you are: sometimes, halfway down, you will find yourself having to develop a different path to your goal and sometimes even an entire adjustment to the goal itself!
7. Drive: this is that one little bit of dissatisfaction with the "here and now" that will urge you to move toward a different aim.
8. Confidence: a huge amount of trust in yourself and whatever else you believe in is required, for that is what will ultimately get you where you want to be.
9. Self-love: you should nurture the awareness that you are doing this all for yourself and that therefore no goal is worth excessively stressing over. The fact that you want to reach that goal is because YOU want it. So, if getting

there is pure hell, why should you proceed? This is when you should jump to . . .

10. Refocus: rethink your goal, reevaluate your possibilities. Then, after formulating your new definition of success, start at point 1 again.

On a more serious note, success also has a lot to do with remaining relatively unscathed in a world where so many things can go wrong. Some call this form of looking at success, reaching a state of nirvana. Sounds pretty far-fetched, but that too depends on how you choose to perceive it. At work, you can attain this by caring about the well-being of others, but not making one's well-being depend on yours. However, this way of being and performing, although sought-after by so many of us because of its guarantee for a peaceful, undisturbed life, is not very easy to achieve. In fact, it seems an almost impossible state to reach for a caring parent, for as long as you have children, and you care for them, you are practically incapable of being content if the children are not doing well in the ways that matter most: health, happiness, and survival.

Yet, aside from the caring issue, which we all have to deal with to a certain extent, we can still achieve success when we make a conscious effort to keep our priorities in order. That is, not attaching yourself to anything that can be taken away again: not a position, not a possession, not even your own life. Yes, that's a deep one, and it is a hard state to achieve, but not impossible, especially when you start seeing things in perspective.

It is all about perspectives, you know. Perspectives are eminent. Perspectives may be considered the biggest business of all. Look around you: there are so many people and institutions that are making staggering fortunes by being in the business of selling perspectives. Some preach the perspective of guilt to place a burden on followers' souls in order to make them submissive. Some lecture the perspective of punishment to impose fear on followers in order to have them refrain from doing certain things. Some promote the perspective of a forthcoming yet distant paradise as a reward to motivate followers in doing the things they want them to do.

And some preach the perspective of developing one's own perspective: Turning inside to obtain insight. They do that by informing others that they are not followers, but entities who should develop their own perceptions; and that they should not feel forced to do anything that is not in harmony with their spirit; that they should only be submissive toward their inner voice, which will tell them what is the right thing to do; that they should only fear this inner voice, sometimes called conscience, as it will be their sole punisher if they wander from their own values; and that they can achieve paradise every day of every year if they maintain respect for the insights they have attained. And these are the ones that ultimately reach the state where they can connect with others, as they have discovered their own source of serenity, and can now care for others without making their ultimate well-being depend on these others. They can practice interconnection because they have achieved inner connection.

So, yes: you can become untouched by detaching yourself from everything that can be taken away; positions, possessions, and even your own life. And yes, even parents with strong emotional ties to their children can reach this state, but it may take longer, and it may require more effort.

And who says anyway that nirvana has to be a constant place to reside? Is life not in and of itself a chain of changes, and thus, a guarantee for ups and downs? And is paradise, or nirvana if you will, then, not an impermanent haven?

Now, for the ones who wonder what the aforementioned explanation about being untouched and developing your own perceptions has to do with the world of work: try to achieve anything while being insecure, unfocused, disconnected from colleagues, and inwardly unbalanced. Success starts with knowing what you want, and can only be reached when you go for what you want. And going for what you want often requires bundled efforts: team spirit. And team spirit requires a spiritual workplace. And a spiritual workplace requires trust and interconnectedness. Now, if success is what you want: your paradise; your nirvana; and you know that it starts with knowing what you want, you may realize by now that knowing what you want requires nothing more than inner connection, which is . . . right: turning inside to obtain insight.

Need I say more?

29

THINKING ABOUT HAPPINESS

HAPPINESS IS . . .

Doing what you love to do
Being where you want to be
Enjoying your life
And not wanting to change
A thing . . .

Smiling without a reason
Liking the current season
Listening to your heart
And cheerfully hearing
It sing . . .

Taking life the easy way
Treasuring it day by day
Being grateful for
What comes and goes
Without a cling . . .

Appreciating here and now
Knowing someway, somehow,
Things are just good
Granting your mood
A jolly swing . . .

~ Joan Marques

Since so many people strive to be happy but claim to be unhappy, let's first look at unhappiness.

What determines unhappiness? The answer to this question could be given in a one-liner: It is the discrepancy between what we can get, and what we really want. Unfortunately, in most cases, what we can get does not equal what we want. And that creates a feeling of dissatisfaction, resulting in unhappiness.

This discrepancy manifests itself in different areas of our life. And depending on how much value we assign to that particular area, our emotional response will vary from slight irritation to major devastation. At work, we may be able to deal with a downturn regarding a certain desired position, and shrug it off while anticipating the next opportunity. In the store we may hesitate, but ultimately let go of that absolutely gorgeous dress and choose a less impressive one, because our finances don't allow the purchase of the one we really want. At the highest, we'll dream about that dress for a few nights, but the pain will be endurable. However, when it comes to the private area of love, the lack of being able to get what we want can become a life-challenging burden.

It seems, though, that some people are more rational than others: they will only go so far to try and get what they desire. If the effort becomes too cumbersome, they will give up and focus their attention elsewhere. How simple, rational, and clever! But then there are those of us who don't give up that easily. Whether that is because of ingrained perseverance, or plain old stubbornness, it becomes a pain that affects the rationality and sobriety of the perseverant.

And the main question remains, what will happen if the goal is finally achieved? What if you find out after all this time that your target was not worth your while? How do you go about dealing with your renewed unhappiness after the first glorious moments have subsided, and the harsh, unfulfilling reality sets in?

In general, even without having done a survey on the topic, I think that there are far more unhappy people in the world than there are ones who consider themselves entirely content. Just look at the escalating trends of dissatisfied workforce members, consider the soaring divorce rates, and think of all the romance- and dating websites, overflowing with people who are searching for a soul mate. All of this makes you wonder if there really is no way for people to learn how to adjust their mindsets and alter their focus when one goal does not seem achievable. Yet, this would straightly contradict with the often given encouragement to "chase your dreams" and "go for what you want." It would also justify the acceptance of mediocrity: if you can't get this, simply lower your standards and go for that! And if that is not achievable, lower a bit further, and go for something less!

Whether we consider it fortunate or not, there will always be people who don't want to go for less than they desire. These are the ones who are known as the persevering kind. And although their endurance is considered a virtue in career and educational regards, it turns into the ultimate source of unhappiness when it concerns their love life. Result: unhappiness, because what they desire does not equal what they can get. Simple, but not so pleasant.

Let's now contemplate on happiness: Have you ever been accused of being a selfish person for chasing your dreams and wanting to achieve them no matter what? Well, I have. And since I always thought of chasing dreams and reaching goals as expressions of determination and perseverance, this bold accusation set me to think. Here was someone telling me that my efforts to achieve my aims were built on egoism!

Suddenly I laid the link between happiness and selfishness. For, isn't everybody ultimately striving for happiness? And doesn't happiness have as many faces as there are people in the world? Isn't happiness tailored to what we expect from life? Think about it: for one happiness may mean being with that one special partner, for another it may consist of being wealthy, and for yet another it may be as much as experiencing serenity.

Happiness is also a moving target: as things and circumstances change in our lives, happiness becomes defined differently. What made you happy 20 years ago may not mean anything anymore to you today. As we change through life, we develop entirely different conditions for happiness now than before.

It is definitely no news either that happiness changes once you have realized one dream. It simply moves on: Another dream replaces the old one, and happiness is once again out of reach. So, the hunt can restart.

So, if happiness is nothing but the realization of our deepest desires; shouldn't we actually cease seeing egoism as something negative and start praising it as the only way progress is being made? Well, perhaps it makes sense to also explain that you have egoism of the enlightened, constructive kind, and egoism of the negative, destructive kind, which is more often referred to as "egotism." Egoism is the moral concept that composes self-interest as the substance of morality while egotism is the excessive focus on oneself based on an unjustified sense of narcissism. Egoism can drive people to work harder and longer than they actually should in order to earn the money they need to realize the materialistic parts of their dreams. Egoism drives people to achieve anything they focus on. Egoism thus leads to success, no matter what you choose your definition of "success" to be.

To me, for instance, success is nothing more than doing what I like: executing my passion. I love being a university professor because I love sharing the knowledge I gained through study and through life's lessons with others, while, at the same time, this knowledge gets enhanced by the bits and pieces these others contribute in the process of knowledge exchanging. I see that as success. I do what I like most, and I do it in a setting that does not tie me to a boring daily schedule, which, to me, would be the epitome of unhappiness. So, since I have achieved that, I feel that I am successful. And happy! Now, how selfish is that?

Some may say, "Very selfish!" And maybe they are right. But if that is true, then selfishness should immediately be liberated from its negative connotation. For selfishness, in that case, is nothing else than "what drives people to achieve their happiness." And a happy world is one where people can stand each other so much better.

The only regrettable note here may be that sometimes the happiness of one person is achieved at the expense of another. Not deliberately, maybe, but still. It may be that two people are striving for the same goal: a desirable partner or a prestigious position at work, for instance. And unfortunately, this partner, or this position, is one and the same entity. Thus, the one who finally succeeds in attracting that partner or position will be successful and happy. The other will not.

A positive way to end this little write-up may be that, fortunately, most of us, human beings, are flexible creatures. That means that we can adapt to change and learn to focus on something new. If one goal turns out to be unachievable, most of us have the suppleness to redefine our desire and go for the newly formulated goal.

So, hurray to egoism (not to be confused with egotism), success, flexibility, and happiness!

30

KEEPING UP WITH TRENDS

With consistent challenges hovering over our global society, and mixed messages of improvement and decline alternating one another, there is a lot for us to rethink. Whether you choose to take on a highly cautious approach or simply perceive any challenge, including the recent COVID-19 pandemic, as part of a recurring wave in line with prior global scares, you simply cannot ignore the social mandates that come along with each new issue.

Within the context of organizations, the challenges for leaders are also multiple and diverse. Consider these:

Shifts in societal values: with the ever-evolving nature of work and the shift to a global knowledge economy, we find higher educated employees in workplaces everywhere, demanding more involvement to feel satisfied (Higgs, 2003). Leaders now regularly have to consider the bigger picture of their performance; increase their tolerance levels for diverse environments; remain focused on their core principles rather than just following every new trend; surround themselves with people who have complementary skills; and expand their horizons, in order to remain abreast of developments and continue excelling (Marques, 2010).

Shifts in investor focus: in contrast to the obsession with revenues and shareholder returns in the previous century, investors are now more interested in the quality and depth of an organization's leader (Higgs, 2003). Corporate reputation has emerged into a discipline of its own, against the backdrop of the numerous ethical scandals and the growing mistrust in leaders' moral standards during the early years of this century (Resnick, 2004). It is clearer than ever that investor trust needs to be restored, and that this needs time and a consistent, attentive exercise of ethics by corporate leaders (Jennings, 2005).

Ability to lead organizational change: Today's leaders have been likened to "generals leading troops across a rugged, unmapped, quake-prone battlefield, against many different armies in a struggle to the death that never ends" (*Developing Agile Leaders*, 2010, p. 12). Therefore, rather than being leery and inhibited toward change, they have to thrive on it. The concept of stability has changed from remaining the same for a long time into flexibly and undauntedly riding the tides of today's corporate sea. In order to perform well, today's leaders have to react quickly; anticipate change, so that they can act proactively; be visionaries and strategists, so that they can be trendsetters rather than followers; perform as role models and set clear goals; promote and rewards agility; hone team performance; and be consistent in their feedback to minimize confusion (*Developing Agile Leaders*, 2010).

The influence of excessive stress on employees: With the increased demands on and changed requirements for organizational performance, the insight has sunk in that employees will perform better and be more committed if they have a leader they trust and have a good relationship with (Higgs, 2003). Workforce members are impacted when stress accumulates. Cumulative stress comes from recurring, unsettled stressful situations, which require an increasing level of personal resilience to manage.

Changes, especially the challenging ones, bring the best and the worst to the surface in people. You will witness unbridled self-centeredness and inconsideration, but also increased levels of care and concern. And those fluctuations are not just limited to professional environments. You can see them everywhere in the community. Reflecting on the early COVID-19 outbreak days, there were viral videos of people who piled toilet paper and kitchen towels in their shopping cards, far beyond their annual needs, and at the dire expense of others who tried to purchase only what they needed. Yet, there were also instances where people demonstrated spontaneous camaraderie, like the case where a woman's credit card declined at the cashiers, and she would have to leave behind all her much-needed purchases. Suddenly one, then two, then several other folks in line decided to chip in toward paying her balance, much to her teary-eyed gratitude.

The end of changes and challenges is not in sight. It never will as long as we live. One trial or tribulation will be followed by another, but that doesn't have to be considered a problem. Quite the contrary: as leaders of ourselves and others, we can decide to perceive the unforeseen encounters of life as opportunities for reinvention and growth (see also the chapters on mental models, adaptability, and creativity).

Here are some perspectives and actions to consider on your path toward facing and succeeding through current and future trends. I labeled them the 5 Gs:

- *Grant those on all sides of the spectrum an opportunity to assist.* Giving people ownership will draw out hidden talents, strengthen their confidence, and establish a stronger bond overall.
- *Get a chance to revalue our social system.* While many of us dream of retirement and staying home all the time, we are now realizing the creativity we'll need to deviate from excessive boredom.

- *Give the environment a break.* With about 75% of the US population being ordered to stay at home, we can vividly imagine the restoration of clean air this brings.
- *Gravitate toward more change acceptance.* Many of us are wondering about the effects of this global pandemic on our social systems. Which trends will disappear and which will emerge? How will that affect us?
- *Gain deeper, change-evoking insight into the things we usually ignore, such as,*

  - *Practicing* more serenity and taking better care of ourselves.
  - *Entertaining* creative ways of keeping ourselves constructively occupied.
  - *Ascertaining* the daily habits of those we share our lives with.
  - *Converting* our established habits of selfish "fun" (including keeping animals captive).
  - *Evaluating* the bigger picture of our life, to assess whether it's time for a change.

There is no better opportunity to reinvent yourself and your circumstances than in times of challenges. You can elect for these days to enter history as a grim episode, or add your own light to any experience by making it as constructive as possible. The choice is yours.

References

George, B., et al. (2010). Developing agile leaders for the 21st century. *People and Strategy*, *33*(4), pp. 12–13.

Higgs, M. (2003). How can we make sense of leadership in the 21st century? *Leadership & Organization Development Journal*, *24*(5), pp. 273–284.

Jennings, M. M. (2005). Ethics and investment management: True reform. *Financial Analysts Journal*, *61*(3), pp. 45–58.

Marques, J. (2010). Inside-out insight: Considerations for 21st century leaders. *Journal of Global Business Issues*, *4*(1), pp. 73–81.

Resnick, J. T. (2004). Corporate reputation: Managing corporate reputation—applying rigorous measures to a key asset. *The Journal of Business Strategy*, *25*(6), pp. 30–38.

31

EMBRACING CHANGE

Every era in history deserves its own credit for the progress it brought. Although you may look back today and wonder how the people in previous centuries managed to get by, it remains important to understand that for them, those were critical times of change, immense challenges, and progress.

Management was still in a developmental stage in the 20th century, and looking back to those times, we can find many learning opportunities, especially when we examine examples of poor management in the early stages of the century. Oftentimes, there was one single style implemented, and usually, that style was heavily task-oriented and not so much people-focused. It was like being forced only to waltz while the world played many kinds of music (Crosby, 1992).

If we look around us, we can see many examples of 20th-century management still in place. There are habits and policies in place in many workplaces that date back to the industrial revolution, even though we have left that era behind us a long time ago. Several organizations are still run as if they perform mechanistic operations and functions; as if processes, occurrences, and challenges are still predictable and measurable; as if our expectations can easily be realized through calculations and predications, and as if there is one single best way to advance (Stumpf, 1995).

Yet, we should not think that it was all bad in earlier times. The 20th century was an impressive one in many ways. In none of the centuries before, over the entire course of human civilization, has there been so much change and progress as in that one. The 20th century brought us a fascinating package of developments and challenges: massive diversity in engineering and appliances, but also destructive world wars, immense growth, and overwhelming losses of human lives. Indeed, the 20th century gave rise to emotions, trends, phenomena, and cultural shifts unknown to humanity before. Progress in that era meant moving forward, but moving forward did not always happen with long-term or even short-term advancements for others in mind. Progress pertained to economic and technological advancement without consideration of moral, environmental, or societal consequences.

Being the bedrock of so many inventions, new trends, and developments, the 20th century brought a major turnaround in the way humanity worked, thought, traveled, shopped, communicated, and perceived power. With the arrival of new possibilities and swifter actions, new threats surfaced as well, and it took some time for some of these treats to become clear. A good example is the use of depleting resources. Not only did abundant ways of consuming cause concern of goods that were now becoming scarcer but also brought health and sustainability threats to the forefront, such as air pollution, global warming, and global climate change.

In the last few decades of the 20th century, change emerged into one of the most powerful concepts in business. Workforce members were made aware that change was the only constant, and that it was occurring at an ever-increasing pace. Every member and every aspect of the corporate chain was subject to speed: speed in innovating to surpass competitors, speed in output to expand market share, and speed in profit generation to keep shareholders satisfied. The quicker a manager could demonstrate an upward trend in the corporation's performance, the more heroic he was considered to be (Tilly, 2003).

Until the last few decades of the 20th century, very few members of the human race were concerned about the impact of their actions on future generations. Corporations were mainly focused on growth and outperforming competitors, which oftentimes meant: finding the most inexpensive resources for the highest possible production to increase market share.

In our day and age, progress is increasingly perceived as growth with consideration of the well-being of stakeholders: immediate and distant, human and nonhuman. Awareness about carbon footprints, environmental responsibility, and spiritual behavior, as advancement strategies, is finally gaining prominence in the aftermath of the turbulent first two decades of the 21st century, with numerous exposures of those who engaged in self-centered progress.

Considering the trends and behaviors that matter today in a world of growing interconnectedness, the following change-aware skills matter today for those who lead or aspire to lead in work environments:

Connection. The will and insight to connect with people and other beings outside of our comfort zone, so that we can learn to understand, respect, and appreciate them, and elevate our readiness to work toward a collaborative coexistence. Understanding our own drives and motives can be instrumental in wanting to understand those of others. We can enhance our self-knowledge in various ways, such as through deep contemplation, and engaging in relaxing, nonwork-related activities, such as walking, gardening, or knitting. All these processes, which are unrelated to our work, help increase our sense of wholeness, thus our self-knowledge and our readiness to connect with others (Pillay, 2016).

Communication. The ability to find ways to learn from and share with others, so that broader awareness arises. Communication does not only happen in verbal ways, but very often even more in nonverbal ways, through which deeper understanding and acceptance can be attained. Some suggestions: keep the messages simple; make assignments interesting and constructive; motivate others, keep response options open, keep it realistic, timely, and appealing (Everse, 2011).

Consideration. This pertains to opening our minds and hearts, so that we may understand what we see, hear, and feel. The quality of communication between leaders and employees is enhanced through the leaders' wisdom, which includes comprehension, acceptance of one another, self-reflection, and compassion (Zacher et al., 2014).

Cooperation and collaboration. The stage where we find ways to undertake constructive action toward betterment for all. Actions don't always lead to success. Sometimes they may have to be undertaken at a small level for quite some time before others will decide to follow. While *cooperation* gets people together to work on a common goal, it is *collaboration* that will enhance efficiency through streamlined and well-attuned operations (Ashkenas, 2015).

Courage. Undertaking action, especially when others don't follow or understand immediately, requires courage. Doing the right things definitely does! To be morally responsible, and making strides toward doing the right thing is not always a popular task. Pfeffer (2011) shares a story of a CEO who experienced this need for courage: it required two months to work toward layoffs, two weeks to implement them, and two years to recover. In hindsight, the layoffs seemed unnecessary in this particular company, but the CEO explained that it was generally expected for him to do what he did. Pfeffer uses this example to demonstrate how tough it can be to act against the status quo.

Confidence. Confidence grows with experience. It also grows when you engage in courageous acts. The great thing with confidence is, that it is contagious, not only toward others, but first and foremost toward yourself. Moss Kanter (2014) explains confidence as an expectation of a positive outcome. Confidence sparks motivation and enhances perseverance toward achieving your goal.

Creativity. Once a goal is set, the need emerges for a large and unexpected dose of creativity to successfully reach it. Moving toward a set goal enhances confidence, which, in turn, can have a positive effect on coming up with creative solutions to unexpected issues. Yet, goals have increasingly become moving targets in our world of rapid changes, continuous surprises, and disruptive trends. Creativity remains a much-praised word, yet a challenging reality in many work settings.

Candidness. Candidness is sometimes unjustly considered to be the gateway to saying hurtful things and damaging relationships. Yet, when people who work together have developed a relationship of trust and constructive interaction, candidness can be a major leap toward progress without barriers.

Compassion. Some feel that compassion should be kept outside organizational doors, because it creates weakness and too much surrendering to employees' needs. Others feel that compassionate leaders get more done due to their ability to relate. Cramm (2010) emphasizes how easy it is for us to fall back into old family or group roles, as we consider them to be expected from us. She warns for the tendency to mentally label others within certain roles without considering them more deeply and thoroughly.

Caution. From a leadership stance, caution has to do with responsible decision-making. When leaders perform in a cautious way, they consider all their stakeholders, and keep in mind that decisions are always made with incomplete information at hand. They ensure that the follow-up to every decision is well-monitored in order to apply adjustments where needed. Caution is one of the important behaviors leaders acquire as they mature.

Care. Caring leaders are valued, even though some sources feel that, like compassion, care should not have a significant place in work environments. Nonetheless, a caring leader can count on his or her employees in challenging times.

Consciousness. Consciousness is frequently described as the ability to subjectively experience wakefulness. Yet, when considered within the realm of a leader's performance, consciousness reaches beyond mere awareness. Rather, it has to do with the leader's ability to observe, digest with the inclusion of experience, stakeholder consideration, and moral responsibility-based reflection, and arrive at a mode of action that seems the most acceptable given the circumstances.

Management practices would not have evolved to today's level if we did not have the past experiences to learn from. The insights shared in this chapter are not negative criticism on the 20th century, but should be seen as a way of evaluating the path that led us to our current, multitiered leadership paradigm. The 12 Cs depicted previously should also not be considered exhaustive, but should be seen as a useful, yet incomplete set of skills and characteristics to be considered by today's and future leaders to ensure greater stakeholder inclusion, and be better prepared for the only constant in today's world, change.

References

Ashkenas, R. (April 20, 2015). There's a difference between cooperation and collaboration. *Harvard Business Review*. Retrieved November 20, 2016, from https://hbr.org/2015/04/theres-a-difference-between-cooperation-and-collaboration.

Cramm, S. (January 11, 2010). Five ways to lead with more compassion. Retrieved November 22, 2016, from https://hbr.org/2010/01/break-free-from-ugly-little-bo.

Crosby, P. B. (1992). 21st century leadership. *The Journal for Quality and Participation, 15*(4), p. 24.

Everse, G. (August 22, 2011). Eight ways to communicate your strategy more effectively. *Harvard Business Review*. Retrieved November 20, 2016, from https://hbr.org/2011/08/eight-ways-to-energize-your-te.

Moss Kanter, R. (January 3, 2014). Overcome the eight barriers to confidence. *Harvard Business Review*. Retrieved November 20, 2016, from https://hbr.org/2014/01/overcome-the-eight-barriers-to-confidence.

Pfeffer, J. (2011). CEOs need courage. *Harvard Business Review*. Retrieved November 20, 2016, from https://hbr.org/2011/09/ceos-need-courage.

Pillay, S. (March 31, 2016). The science behind how leaders connect with their teams. *Harvard Business Review*. Retrieved November 20, 2016, from https://hbr.org/2016/03/the-science-behind-how-leaders-connect-with-their-teams.

Stumpf, S. A. (1995). Applying new science theories in leadership development activities. *The Journal of Management Development, 14*(5), pp. 39–49.

Tilly, C. (2003). *The Politics of Collective Violence* (p. 55). Cambridge University Press, Cambridge.

Zacher, H. H., Pearce, L. L., Rooney, D. D., & McKenna, B. B. (2014). Leaders' personal wisdom and leader-member exchange quality: The role of individualized consideration. *Journal of Business Ethics, 121*(2), pp. 171–187.

32

MAINTAINING BALANCE

JUST BE GOOD

I have reasons to worry but I don't
In the past I would have—now I won't
The lessons learned in recent years were great
I learned that concern before the time is a useless trait
We worry mostly because we cannot see tomorrow
But in hindsight we realize the futility of our sorrow
All efforts in the world cannot provide any guarantee

For whatever is supposed to be—will be
Our book has been written with conscientious finesse
The outcome is set—whether we stress more or less
While we should not sit around idly and wait passively
We should trust in the goodness of the powers that be

Our best is the best thing we can do
Nice times will come when grim ones are through
Problems get solved in the most unexpected way
Blessings surface on the least predicted day
So, I'm not worried if the future looks a bit bleak
Why should I allow this issue to make me weak?

> That future is not here yet
> So why should I fret?
> Who knows what it's good for?
> Who knows where I will be?
> Who knows what may be in store?
> Who knows what we'll see?
> God opens windows when he closes doors
> Just be good—and goodness will be yours . . .
>
> ~ *Joan Marques*

The hectic journey of proving and improving ourselves oftentimes takes such a high toll on us that we hardly find time to lead a fulfilling private life, let alone to reflect on the purpose and sensibility of our path. As we go from day to day, we fall into a sleepwalk pattern, whereby we just go through the motions without taking some distance to evaluate whether these are the actual motions that will lead us to where we want to be. In order to get an idea of the big picture, it is critical to force ourselves now and then to stop, take a few mental steps back, and look at our activities. And this is exactly where the challenge lies: we rarely feel that we have time to do so. We fear that, while we take time to evaluate, others may be racing past us, and cease the opportunities that could have been ours.

It is exactly due to the previous cyclical movements, which so many of us can relate to, that life intervenes, whether we like it or not. These life interventions often appear as undesired events, better known as setbacks. Right at the peak of our performance, we may lose our job, get confronted with death of a loved one, personal illness, or divorce. Whatever the form is in which the setback manifests itself, it forces us to stop what we are doing, and focus on something we had not anticipated before. However, in that process, we often get a chance to take a hard look at the past months or years of our life, and come to surprising conclusions.

Let us use this space to review some exercises that can help you identify your personal balance between ambition and acceptance. We will present three simple, yet effective practices: Daily Reflection Cycle, and Prayer and Meditation.

Daily Reflection Cycle

A great exercise that can become a constructive and insightful habit is to engage in reflection at the end of each day. This reflection exercise can be done individually or with a trusted partner. Ask yourself:

1. What went right today?

   - What contributed to this "right" notion?
   - How did you feel?

- Who benefitted from it?
- What are you most grateful for regarding this occurrence?

2. What could have been better?

- Why do you feel it could be better?
- How do you feel?
- Who was hurt/harmed?
- What can you learn from this in order to prevent it from happening again?
- What good thing(s) came out of this? (list as many as possible)

For major windfalls:

- What happened?
- What is the purpose of this happening?
- Why do I think I deserve this?
- Who should I thank?
- Who should I include in the windfall and why?
- What has changed in my life?
- What are some potential downsides to this windfall?
- Down to earth reminder: this too shall pass.

For major setbacks:

- What happened?
- What is the purpose of this happening?
- Why might I need this experience?
- Could this have been avoided? If so, how?
- Who should I protect in this situation?
- What has changed in my life?
- What are five (or more) "good things" that came from this setback?
- Down to earth reminder: this too shall pass.

Critical reflection on habits, assumptions, and beliefs (can be done alone or in small groups):

1. Consider an assumption, belief, or habit that you have adhered to for a long time.
2. How did it make its way into your life?
3. What do you like about it?
4. What do you dislike about it?
5. Does this belief or habit fulfill you?

- If so, how and why?
- If not, why not?

6. Is this assumption, belief, or habit good for your body, mind, or spirit? How or how not?
7. What do you plan to do about it?
8. List your action plan based on the answer to point 7.

Prayer and Meditation

Prayer and meditation are two very personal ways of establishing and nurturing our inner connection and keeping our focus intact. Each of these activities has the potential to calm us from hectic mindsets and activities, and help us to regain our mental and emotional composure.

Prayer

Prayer is, and will remain, an important way of reflecting on current and future directions and sustaining positive thought. Prayer can be done in groups, or alone. It can be done in a formal and informal setting. In other words, you can pray however and wherever you are. Those among us that are open about their way of praying admit that they pray in the most unlikely moments and circumstances. Prayer is an intimate conversation we have with a higher being that each of us perceives in his or her own way. Yet, whether we believe that this higher being is externally located or right inside of us, we usually pray in silence and lay our concerns before this invisible being, in hopes that we may be granted the insight to engage in the most appropriate course of action. Prayer oftentimes brings about a more peaceful mindset, and with such a mind we have the ability to make more rational and well-intended decisions. Prayer can help us see our blind spots and restore our sense of doing the right thing, toward others as well as to ourselves.

Meditation

Meditation has become an increasingly popular term in the past decade or so, as Western people open up to alternative ways of getting in touch with their core. Meditation transcends the boundary of talking to a higher being. It is very personally oriented, and can also be done in many settings: in groups, alone, in formal and informal locations. Just as with prayer, there are multiple types of meditation: religious-based and nonsectarian. The one we consider most appropriate for internal balance restoration is insight meditation or Vipassana. Vipassana is not religious in foundation, so it can be practiced by religious and nonreligious people without any concern. Vipassana is generally acknowledged as the meditation technique Gautama Siddhartha, generally known as "the Buddha" engaged in when he became enlightened. It was due to the Vipassana practice of turning inward that the Buddha gained critical insight in his existence, the workings of cause and effect, and the destructive workings of mental biases (Snelling, 1991).

Vipassana meditation consists of four progressive steps:

1. Slow scan: This step consists of moving your attention, ever so slowly, from the top of your head to the tip of your toe and back. You deliberately focus on every part of your body that your mind observes, and leave no piece unexamined.
2. Free flow sweep: At this stage, you sweep your attention as a whole up and down the body, with more attention to areas that respond less to the sensations you feel.
3. Spot check: Inspecting, with your mind, a few parts of your body, and becoming aware of the sensations this brings. Once you have done a few spot checks, you can continue scanning and sweeping.
4. Penetrating and piercing: At this stage, you move to a more intense level of examining, from the external sweep and scan to an internal mental penetration, thus examining the inside of the body as well. Because this is a more advanced step, practitioners may want to first do this under guidance of a Vipassana teacher, or by attending one of the many (non-charging) Vipassana centers worldwide (Marques & Dhiman, 2009).

Practicing Vipassana meditation ignites personal awareness and awakens us about the impermanence of everything, including ourselves. Once we absorb that awareness deeply, we become abundantly aware of the uselessness of entitlement, pettiness, holding grudges, and other negative emotions. In fact, Vipassana aims to make us aware of the damage that both craving and aversion have on us. As ambitious people, we crave possessions and positions, and by doing so, disrupt our peace of mind. We want to fulfill our ambition once we have identified and labeled it, and we set out to do so, sometimes at the expense of others' or our own serenity. Similarly, we hold aversions to some people, tasks, and things, and by doing so, disturb our inner calm, and dwell on negative thought patterns that negatively affect our mental, and sometimes also our physical wellness.

Vipassana enables meditators to gain mastery over the mind on the basis of morality and to develop experiential wisdom to eradicate all the defilements of craving and aversion (Goenka, 2001). Vipassana meditation helps us understand how the mind can influence the body. It also enhances our awareness of our dependency on pleasant situations and the craving we develop for them, as well as our aversion to the painful experiences life places on our path. Vipassana can be a critical path to releasing both the cravings and the aversions, particularly in areas where they infringe on our peace of mind, enhance our stress levels, and ignite or amplify a sense of misery.

The two balance-initiating practices described in this chapter are just a small minority in the heap of so many more at your disposal. Hopefully, you will discover what works best for you.

References

Goenka, S. N. (2001). *Was the Buddha a Pessimist?* (p. 62). Vipassana Research Institute, Dhammagiri, Igatpuri.

Marques, J., & Dhiman, S. (2009). Vipassana meditation as a path toward improved management practices. *Journal of Global Business Issues, 3*(2), pp. 77–84.

Snelling, J. (1991). *The Buddhist Handbook: The Complete Guide to Buddhist Schools, Teaching, Practice, and History.* Inner Traditions International, Rochester, VT.

33

THOSE DIFFICULT PEOPLE

Have you ever entered an office where you feel as if you're being looked away, even if everybody smiles at you? I guess we all have. It's bad enough if you have to be at such an office on a regular basis for deliveries or other work-related appointments. But what if you work in that office and have to deal with the sensation of being looked away by colleagues in order to ensure your monthly paycheck?

The funny thing about this feeling—which, by the way may be more familiar to women than men for some reason—is, that it is nothing more than that: a feeling. You cannot put your finger on the roots of it, and it's pretty hard to rationalize. It is an intuitive matter, but it's there! For sure! Another interesting detail of this situation is, that it is, unfortunately, more often than not created by women, and perhaps therefore also mainly experienced by women. Whether this is due to their protective instinct coming forth from enormous struggles to get where they are, or just a lingering sense of insecurity, women have a tendency to emotionally mark their territory in a way that others may not be able to define, but will certainly feel.

If you care to take a closer look into one of those typical territorial workplaces, you will find that there is often one leader, and a group of followers who show unconditional devotion to this territory protector. Because it is such a subtle power scene, every new entrant will have to figure it out on his or her own.

Male entrants seem to have less trouble with it, either because they have a harder time picking up the vibes from high levels of subtlety, or because they are not treated as potential competitors in the political arena.

Female entrants, on the other hand, will quickly find out who is the real boss in that work environment, aside from all title plates. Once their intuition has led them in finding that out, they have two options in dealing with it:

1. They can obey the existing monarchy and become submissive.
2. They can ignore it and become an outcast.

Choosing for option 2 is practically impossible if you have to be in the territorial workplace on a daily basis.

It is more easily applicable if you only have to show your face now and then. Most female employees will therefore choose for option 1, because it is the only way to survive in such a workplace. The choice between the two aforementioned options is often also determined by character and position: a woman with a confrontational nature will most likely not linger in this work environment for too long, especially if she is not interested in powerhouses, or wants to be the leader herself. In the latter case, she will probably switch jobs until she finds herself a work environment where she can establish her own monarchy.

A woman with a high level of education will probably be less interested in the monarchy system and will ignore it even though she will be aware of it. She can afford to remain an outcast because of her credentials, which make her important to the performance of the organization as a whole. If she proves herself to the organization, she may be endured, but will never become part of the in-group. If she doesn't prove herself, she will be forced out with every available emotional weapon.

In case you are yet to encounter this phenomenon, here are some points to enlighten your perspective. These are some of the signs that you are in a territorial workplace:

*   You find, after a few visits, that you have to take a deep breath to boost up your dignity before you open the door to the office.
*   You feel as if you need to make yourself invisible in order not to disturb the existing peace and quiet.
*   You start sweating when you need to ask someone something, even if work-related.
*   You find yourself speaking soft, quick, and maybe even in a stumbling way, although you may be very eloquent under other circumstances.
*   You heave a sigh of relief when you can finally leave the place. And "finally" always seems so far away!

All of these emotions (I call them "intruder-awareness sensations") exist, even if you genuinely love the kind of work you're doing! Now, do you still wonder why working from home has become increasingly popular, and, what's more striking, has been listed as the most desirable way for women to work? Most likely not.

One important detail of succeeding in work environment with "difficult" characters is to make sure you perform excellently. What distinguishes excellent performers from average ones? The answers to this question vary from "greater perseverance" and "enhanced resilience," to "more creativity," "increased adaptability," and "a higher tolerance level," and "a thicker skin." However, the prime factor is the decision to utilize your qualities constructively.

In principle, everybody wants to make an impression. Graffiti, tree- and sidewalk carvings, screaming tattoos, multiple piercing, or odd hair colors are done because somebody wants to draw attention to themselves and stand out. Making a difference is hard enough as it is. But making a *positive* difference, especially in a territorial workplace, is even harder. Many people lack the willpower to utilize their positive qualities for constructive purposes. Life beats most of us down hard enough to drive us to a point where making a positive difference seems impossible. So, we either grow numb and submit to mediocrity or flip to the other side. What can you do to ensure personal and professional excellence under all circumstances? It's FOCUS, which is not only a great way of ensuring your concentration toward accomplishing your goals but is also used as an acronym in this chapter.

- **F**ormulate your goal. Plan around the one thing you want to be remembered for. Make sure it's something you will be proud of—whether it is geared toward impressing the world or just your neighborhood. Be flexible in formulating your goal.
- **O**rganize a realistic strategy toward your goal. Set a reasonable timeframe toward the ultimate target. Flexibility in your strategy and your goal may be wise. Don't just aim in one single direction. The narrower your strategy, the greater your chance of failing. Build in alternative routes, even alternative destinations. You may aspire to act, for instance, but what if you turn out to be more successful as a director?
- **C**lassify intermediate goals: the baby steps that are easily achieved and that you can be proud of and celebrate on your way to the final destination. Acknowledge small victories and reward yourself for achieving them.
- **U**ndertake action. Every goal requires mastering specific qualities and overcoming hurdles on your path. That's where your strength is tested. But imagine how proud you'll be when you overcome a challenge. You may have to undertake various actions—education and internships—and nurture skills— patience, energy, endurance, networking, reading—to get where you want to be. But don't give up.
- **S**tudy. Reflect regularly. Find out if your goal needs adjustment, if it still gives you the thrill it once did, and if you still consider it worth your while. You need these moments to ensure that you're not wasting precious time and efforts. Yet, don't confuse setbacks with goal derailment; challenges can cause you to question your goal and your ability to achieve it. Separate transitory disappointments from structural disassociation with your focus.

Working with difficult people is not pleasant, but you could perceive it as a great experience to boost your spine. Let us illustrate the philosophy behind this notion with a story. In a course there were 20 students, all living on the premises, as the location was rather far outside of town. Nineteen students were very attentive and serious, but one was a real pain, disrupting the sessions, bullying his peers, and sometimes even stealing some of their goods. One day, the teacher had to leave for a few days. The 19 "good" students saw their chance to finally get rid of the difficult student. They made his life so miserable that he left. Upon the teacher's return, he counted the heads and immediately asked where the 20th student was. The 19 good students told him they got rid of him, so now the lessons could finally be conducted with peace and dignity. The next day, however, the teacher left unexpectedly, only to return a few days later with . . . the "difficult" student. The 19 others were very upset and asked the teacher why he brought the disrupting character back into their midst. The teacher responded: "I brought him back, because he serves an important purpose in your lives. If he is not here, who will teach you endurance, patience, tolerance, and excellence under stress?"

34

DEALING WITH SETBACKS

TIMES

There are times
When my heart feels frozen
While my feet seem to be stuck
On hot coal

When the smile
That lights up my face
Is in absolute stark contrast
With my soul

When the days
Arduously twine together
As rusty strings
On a chain

And the sun,
In spite of all its brightness,
Yields the same effect
As the rain

When wisdom
And spiritual reasoning

> Bring very little relief
> To my mood
>
> And I have to
> Do my upper-level best
> To keep in mind that
> Life is good
>
> ~ *Joan Marques*

From the concert of life, no one gets a script: an old adage that comes to mind every time unexpected things happen, especially if these are of a disappointing nature. Disappointments never come alone. Like cowards, they arrive in pairs, and very often even as trios. Even if you are aware that things will get better, it remains dreadful to face setbacks. Your natural sense of optimism may be stellar, yet, you are still very likely to experience an initial sense of gloom when a setback hits. This is normal because human beings are creatures of habit, so they usually mourn during transitions, sometimes even when those transitions lead to progress! The process of mourning pertains to leaving an old, familiar situation behind, and moving toward a new one that is still largely unfamiliar.

One thing to keep in mind is that every setback holds a strong message and a powerful opportunity. You just have to be willing to face it, and consider your options. What will you do next? How could you move out of the situation you landed in without too much damage? Is there an opportunity to move to a more constructive situation after the setback? Here are some questions you can ask yourself to start the recovery process after a setback:

1. What is/are the lesson(s) I can learn from this experience?

    Make sure you don't just look on the surface, but consider the bigger picture as well. If your setback is a discontinuation of a daily or weekly trend, for instance, you could think about the need to move into new directions and moving to a higher plane of development as some of your lessons. If your perceived setback pertains to a change in your work situation, you could consider that things may not have seemed the way they looked and that you should focus on the future instead of standing still or looking back.

2. What were the things I did not enjoy about the old situation?

    There are upsides and downsides to every situation. Even the nicest chore has some less pleasant angles to it. Yet, when we lose something, we think it was the best we ever had, just because it is no longer available. A situation that has now ceased to exist may lose some of that embellished desirability if you consider its good and bad elements, thus refrain from over-romanticizing it. This is how you keep yourself from agonizing too much about a situation you cannot restore anyway.

3. What are some new avenues I could try, now that this setback is a fact?

    Life always offers us choices. Not all options may be as desirable, but there will definitely be some that are worth pursuing. Start thinking, as soon as you have digested the first blow. Make a list of options, if you can. Even if some of the alternatives you write down seem ridiculous, don't give up on them too quickly. A slight modification may change an initially ludicrous sounding idea into something perfectly viable. It may take a while before this modification enters your mind, which is why you should consider your alternatives regularly.

4. How can I get started on the new path?

    Begin with small steps. Don't get too zealous too soon. But start and try as soon as you regain your natural energy. The first attempts may not lead to anything, but sooner or later, you will find your new focus.

There are great self-leadership opportunities in setbacks. The very act of engaging in self-reflection, as suggested previously, and the subsequent preparation of an action plan, followed by the action itself, is a manifestation of leadership. Even when it feels like the entire world is against you, there is one person who should not let you down, and that is the leader inside you.

A plus side to all of this is that there are always people who observe you, even when you think they don't. People choose their leaders on the basis of their actions, not necessarily on basis of their positions. If you can prove that you are able to guide yourself out of precarious situations, others may decide to follow you, even if only as a role model for their actions.

35

THE NEED TO GET OUT (OF YOUR COMFORT ZONE)

Why do so many organizations descend into mediocrity after decades of great success? The answer is as simple as the solution is difficult: because they are led by human beings, and human beings, by nature, don't like change. As a consequence, these organizations are averse to change as well, and they dwell in markets that were once flourishing but have now become saturated, disinterested, or perhaps even nonexistent. They sell products that have either become obsolete or are in desperate need of a transformation.

However, when leaders dare to step out of their comfort zones, ensure a dynamic workforce, and teach this workforce the advantages of making bold but responsible decisions, lasting excellence can be secured for their organizations. Stepping out of your comfort zone is a major challenge because we all prefer to do things the easy way whenever they think we can get away with it. The problem is the easy way has gradually become a less and less viable choice.

Now that we're all part of a global workforce and a global market, whether we realize and want it or not, opportunities as well as complications have increased. We have more options, but so do our competitors. And those competitors emerge from the most unexpected places. Change is on its way again while we're still adapting to the last new thing. Because stepping out of the comfort zone is such a challenge, people should consider ways, first, to remain aware of this challenge and, second, to do something about it. There are various actions you can take to get yourself out of your comfort zone.

Here are five of them; you can use them whether you are a business owner, a company manager, or just an individual who wants to live life to the fullest.

1. Read something different at least once a month. This action is borrowed from leadership guru Tom Peters. In his book *The Brand You50: Fifty Ways*

to Transform Yourself from an "Employee" into a Brand That Shouts Distinction, Commitment, and Passion!, Peters encourages people to visit a shop and pick up a few magazines they have never read before. This idea makes a lot of sense because it exposes people to new worlds that they are usually not a part of. They read and see different things, and different is what gets the creative juices flowing.

2. Have lunch with someone outside your regular circle of friends and business associates. This action is also inspired by Peters' book. Try to do this at least once every other month. Keep a database of the contact information of all the interesting people you come across and access this database regularly. All kinds of fascinating ideas and information can emerge from these refreshing lunch appointments.

3. Travel. Visit another country at least once every other year. You'll be exposed to other cultures and ways of living. As a result, you'll absorb new ideas even when you're not looking for them. And you'll become more familiar with options, which breaks down the fear-related boundaries that some people face because they never leave their geographical comfort zones.

4. Surf the Internet to keep yourself abreast of what's going on in your area of interest. Make sure you don't stick to the familiar sites. Break the routine. Stepping out of one's comfort zone is a major challenge for anyone because people tend to prefer to do things the easy way. Google the topic of your interest and visit some sites you've never visited before. They may provide you with some new perspectives.

5. Reflect. Do some intense self-searching at least once per quarter. For instance, you might ask yourself, "Do I currently have what it takes to achieve the future I envision?" If you answer no, then ask yourself how you need to improve and take action to make the improvements. If you answer yes, then ask, "Could I obtain an advantage over others?" If you answer yes to that, then develop a strategy to obtain the advantage. If you answer no, start considering alternatives.

Be critical while asking yourself these questions. Assure yourself that you're not settling for less today compared with yesterday because of an aversion to change. Many people justify their indolence by raising arguments like these: "This is just a temporary depression of the market in which we operate. It will get better in a while." "The lower performance today is due to unrealistic profits in the past; the market is finally balancing out." "If you think we're doing badly, look at so-and-so—they're doing even worse!"

These are some of the standard defenses people use to protect the status quo and refrain from getting out of their comfort zone. Remember, if you want to get ahead you should step up your performance by considering the performance of those who are performing splendidly, even if you think they're out of your league. While this seemingly contradicts a statement made in another chapter ("Stop

Comparing"), it should be noted that you can still look at the performance of others, more as a motivating factor than a source of self-violation. Everyone needs role models. So, why not go for the very best? Aiming high with your aspirations is not a bad thing. Just keep yourself from being reactive instead of proactive. Don't wait for things to happen before changing; instead, be the change that others have to keep up with. If you delay changing until things get really bad, you've waited too long, and a recovery may be impossible. Stay away from the comfort zone. It will pay off.

Reference

Peters, T. (1999). *The Brand You50: Fifty Ways to Transform Yourself From an "Employee" Into a Brand That Shouts Distinction, Commitment, and Passion!* Alfred A. Knopf, Inc, New York, NY.

36

EMBRACING "DIFFERENT"

Discontinuity is more a requirement than an exception in the pursuit of a successful life these days. In every field of activity, there are numerous examples of the interconnectedness between success and being different, whereby "being different" pertains to applying radical changes to the status quo.

More and more business gurus refer to radicalism as the outstanding—no, the *only* way—to success. At the personal level, Tom Peters (1999) encourages his readers in "*The Brand You 50*" (also mentioned in the previous chapter) to do some thorough self-examination in order to find out how they can be different; to discover the fields in which they distinguish themselves from others. At the business level, Gary Hamel discusses this issue in his book "*Leading the Revolution*," in which he calls for companies to be "revolution-ready," introducing terms such as "nonlinear" and "discontinuous" innovation. Hamel emphasizes on the absolute importance for business organizations to attract visionaries who have the ability to transform businesses into "Gray-haired Revolutionaries." Gray-haired Revolutionaries, then, are "companies that have managed to reinvent themselves *and* their industry more than once" (Hamel, 2000, p. 209). Others have also discussed the power of radicalism in several pieces of literature. Kaplan (1999) rightfully states, "Substantial growth over the long horizon requires discontinuous innovation—disruptive technologies, radical innovations and discontinuities that permit entire industries and markets to emerge" (p. 16).

Of course, you should also realize that not every radical change is necessarily a good one. In fact, what many don't consider is the reality that every seemingly "overnight" success has been preceded by years of trying and failure. There are numerous books out there, written by today's immortally successful people about their broad collection of humiliating slides and slips and their painstaking efforts to get up again before they reached the point that their star rose to the sky.

Being radical is risky. Risk-averse people will not easily go for significant change. It has, by the way, been examined and proven through the years that human beings are risk-averse by nature, and therefore, also change-averse. It's the same problem that withholds organizations from, for instance, encouraging diversity in the workplace: people tend to hold on to what they know. The unknown is a source of fear. Members of another "culture" (which can be race, ethnicity, generation, or anything else that's different) require more time, money, and effort to understand, and the risk for failure in collaborating with them is therefore greater. Of course success, if reached in this setting, will be much greater as well! However, since we all feel best in our "comfort zone" of familiarity, we have a tendency to stick to that, even if success is mediocre with similar people and established processes.

Another problem with applying discontinuity is the fact that it impinges on established and therefore convenient patterns. Imagine the CEO who has led the company to its current level and is now on the edge of retirement. It is likely that he will try to influence the choice of his successor, and thereby will ensure that his style will be continued. He might persist in doing this, even if he was once a radical innovator himself!

So being different is powerful. But what's powerful is not easy. It requires a forceful change of perceptions and habits. It requires bravery. And it requires something that is often perceived by our surroundings as temporary insanity. Many people who dared to do something entirely different in their life have had to break through established personal patterns. Oftentimes they look back at their visionary act as a deed that represents a part of them they were previously unaware of. It is, in hindsight, as much an astonishing experience to them as it is to their environment. That may explain why so many of us—when it comes to drastic changes—are "*incidentalists*," and why, as Hamel states in his aforementioned book, Silicon Valley is full of the bones of one-time visionaries. After all, it takes a lot of guts to make more than one giant step in your life.

In my own opinion, it takes a lot of courage, but helps immensely to:

- Get used to *uncertainty*.
- Have *no expectations* about tomorrow.
- Be in *constant awe* of everything that reveals itself to you.
- Maintain a sense of *naiveté* within.
- *Detach* yourself from your material belongings.

It is only when you transcend the fear of losing the status quo that you will be able to advance to other levels without looking back.

Mama Cass Elliot once sung: "*Different is hard, different is lonely, different is trouble for you only; different is heartache, different is pain, but I'd rather be different than be the same*" . . . How right!

So be *different*. Even if it will raise eyebrows. Even if it will make others wonder about you and your choices. Even if it will estrange you from some of the people you value most. Because it feels so good when ultimately you can look back at your life and *know*—like Hamel (2000) stated it—that you managed to leave your fingerprints on your own (and maybe also your organization's) future.

References

Hamel, G. (2000). *Leading the Revolution*. Harvard Business School Press, Boston, MA.

Kaplan, S. M. (1999). Discontinuous innovation and the growth paradox. *Strategy & Leadership, 27*(2), pp. 16–21.

Peters, T. (1999). *The Brand You 50* (5th ed.). Alfred A. Knopf, Inc, New York, NY.

37

LIFELONG LEARNING AND LEADERSHIP PARADIGMS

As a leadership coach of current and upcoming workforce members, I often find myself placed before the challenge of instigating a series of paradigm shifts. In this chapter, I would like to focus on five of these.

Paradigm shift no. 1: The general perception of leadership. Most people see leadership as an external influence process with three steady elements at its core: a leader, one or more followers, and a situation. What many don't consider, however, is the fact that the process can only be successful externally if it has first been kindled internally. Only when you acknowledge, nurture, and respect your inner leader, can you exude enough confidence and stability to others, so they might decide to follow you.

Paradigm shift no. 2: The specific perception of a leader. Not every person in a supervisory position is accepted as a leader per se. People land in influential positions for a multiplicity of reasons: through promotion or by being hired into an assigned supervisory position, through affiliation with a power source, or through particular knowledge, to name a few. Yet, fulfilling those positions doesn't automatically make them leaders. A leader doesn't necessarily have to hold a supervisory position in any setting. Real leaders can fulfill the most modest roles in work and life, but their leadership mindset attracts others to trust, respect, listen to them, and ask them for advice. And isn't that what leaders are expected to do?

Paradigm shift no. 3: Leaders are both born and made. *Born*, because the very process of conception seals your fate as a leader: what has ultimately become "you" was once the fastest sperm in about 100 million to penetrate an ovulated egg. That in and of itself is a heroic and promising start. *Made*, because you develop traits in the course of your life, and acquire skills and insights that become instrumental in your decision-making processes and your overall behavior. When perceived that way, the mystery of leaders being born or made is quickly dismantled.

Paradigm shift no. 4: Learnability of leadership. There are many books, theories, and courses about leadership, and many of these can be very effective, but they cannot teach you leadership. They can, at best, encourage you to think of yourself as a leader, and inspire you to hone your traits and skills in order to exhibit leadership in your actions from here onward. Whether or not you really take on that challenge and work yourself up to meet ambitious goals is entirely up to you, your self-perspective, and the circumstances you land in, many of which are the results of choices you made at some point in your life.

Paradigm shift no. 5: Realizing the ebbs and flows in leadership performance. Leadership is like a saw: if you don't sharpen it, it gets dull. It's like a mirror: if you don't polish it, it becomes smudged. It's a constant process of working on yourself. That internal exercise that ignites leadership should not be ceased: maintaining your confidence, doing what you need to maintain your leadership self-concept, continuing to propel yourself toward achievements that make you proud inside, and most of all: staying awake. With staying awake I mean: engaging in regular self-reflection and inspection to find out where and how you can improve, whether you are still on the right track, whether there are areas in your life that you need to change, and whether your actions are constructive toward yourself as well as all stakeholders involved.

Considering or even adopting these five paradigm shifts of leadership may not necessarily make you a leader, but they can inspire you to rethink the way you perceived yourself and a number of the people with whom you interact in a wide range of performance areas. Leadership remains a fascinating topic because it is dynamic, multispectral, and therefore protean and personal. Most importantly, leadership is a lifelong learning process, which is only possible toward others after it has started within.

38

ABOUT CREATIVITY

Unless you just returned from a multi-decade trip to outer space, you are probably aware of the quest for creativity that drives today's professional performance. Terms such as creative, motivated, innovative, and problem solving are so clichéd that coaches have advised deleting them from LinkedIn® profiles. There may be good reasons, however, to keep these terms in curriculum vitae and professional profiles.

With the shift from the industrial revolution to the knowledge era, the emphasis on qualities and skills transitioned, too. Although the United States became a manufacturing giant during World Wars I and II, this trend reached maturation in the late 1960s and then gradually spun into decline. Consequently, manufacturing and product assembly shifted from industrial nations to upcoming economies such as China and India. Education became the focus point in Western nations, causing productivity there to move from hands to heads. Meanwhile, the eastern nations have made significant strides and now are marching vigorously toward a shared leadership position in cultivating creative resources. Although we now may have arrived at the brink of yet another era, our affiliation with creative thinking and innovation will most likely remain critical—even if the way we refer to these skills changes.

This chapter considers two levels of nurturing creative minds—personal and organizational—to emphasize the importance of both and highlight their common areas as well as the different approaches needed to bring them to fruition. Finally, there is a discussion reflecting briefly on the interdependency between creativity and innovation.

Personal Aspects

The following areas are critical components that support an individual's ability and willingness to think creatively:

- Source of motivation. When reflecting on individuals' creative skills, we are dealing with a wide variety of levels and manifestations. Whether we consider ourselves creative or are seen by others as such is closely related to motivation levels. There are intrinsically and extrinsically motivated people. Those who are intrinsically motivated are self-starters and more focused on their passions and purposes. They have a higher level of self-understanding and detect early in life what they want to do and what they would rather avoid doing. Extrinsically motivated people, however, are mainly led by incentives created by others. Money, promotion, material gain, or other advancements are their main drivers; without external stimuli, they often lack the willpower to engage in a given activity.

A person with high intrinsic motivation is more likely to display a greater level of creativity because he/she becomes so involved in what's being done, according to Mihaly Csíkszentmihályi (2008) in his pioneering book, *Flow*.

- Meditation. Meditation has long been shunned by various groups as an Eastern-originated practice. Fortunately, meditation is gaining wider acceptance—even in business schools and corporate workplaces. Those who meditate regularly understand that it calms the mind and enables the practitioner to tap into areas of the psyche that were previously inaccessible due to the noise of everyday life.
- Art endeavors. If this chapter was written 30 years ago, this section probably would not have been included. Fortunately, there is increasing awareness of the positive interplay of a balanced diet—whether physical or mental. For our mental diet, exposure to artistic expressions or engagement in artistic endeavors may have a very fertile effect on creative thinking.
- Pursuit of different paths. Tom Peters (1999), author of *The Brand You 50*, recommends doing something different on a regular basis: asking an unlikely colleague to lunch; stepping into an unlikely corner in the bookstore; or exploring different types of books, magazines, or media programs. Doing something outside of the routine will open our eyes to other things and may expand our mental horizons.
- Confidence and optimism. The worst enemy of creative thinking is lack of confidence because it breeds fear, and fear restrains any project. Dickson (2003) shared that scientists who are confident produce more output; even if all their output isn't as good as desired, their confidence drives them forward and they keep producing. Dickson concluded that creative geniuses produce good and bad results, and mentioned Thomas Edison and William Shakespeare as two famous examples of people who are known for great, timeless contributions to humanity—despite their immense number of unacceptable creations. The key is to keep up a positive spirit in spite of failure because the more failures we experience, the greater the chance that we will strike gold in the end.

Organizational Aspects

The organization's approach to managing the workplace environment also has a significant influence on employees' creativity, as described subsequently:

- Workplace spirituality. Not to be confused with religion, the application of a more spiritual mindset lies at the foundation of fueling creative thinking. Spirituality in the workplace is about employees and workplaces seeing work as a spiritual path rather than just a way to earn paychecks. Spiritual workers see work as an opportunity to meaningfully connect, grow, and contribute to society rather than advancing at the expense of others. In an environment where people feel appreciated and where managers nurture mutual acceptance, respect, and understanding, there will be less inhibition and more ownership (Marques et al., 2007).
- Recognition and rewards. Recognition is another no brainer when it comes to creativity; when we are aware that we are properly acknowledged for our accomplishments, we become more proactive in our work and feel more encouraged to share creative ideas in the workplace (Robinson, 2010). If managers want employees to become more creative, they must understand the cycle of interrelated notions that can nourish or kill creativity at work (Perakis, 2011). There are still too many managers who capitalize on extrinsic rewards and ignore the value of intrinsic recognition. Different strokes are needed for different folks, so it is critical for a manager to know what drives the members of his/her workforce.
- Multiple frames and mental models. Bolman and Deal (2008) discuss four frames through which managers and their workforces can review workplace issues in order to perceive the situations from multiple angles and try to solve them in the most appropriate way. They introduce the structural, human resource, political, and symbolic frames. Although these are a great basis for reviewing any corporate concern, they are not the only ones. Creative insights should help us identify which frames are most appropriate for the unique experiences of a given workplace. There may be an IT frame or an emotional intelligence frame, which are more suitable for approaching a specific problem.

Peter M. Senge (2006) introduced mental models, the notion that we all have a unique way of perceiving the world around us. Awareness of different mental models—especially in the workplace—can be a great boost to creative output. Once we lay to rest the tendency to assume that our reality is the only one that exists, we can start engaging in a highly rewarding exchange of perspectives with our coworkers. This leads to a number of frames for viewing any issue and an increased level of creativity for addressing the situation.

- Revival space. Almost two decades ago, Edward de Bono (1988) wrote an article in which he referred to the importance of providing time and space to stimulate creative thinking. He warned that brainstorming sessions were highly overrated and usually didn't deliver any serious creative output. He also cautioned that creative thinking should not be considered the virtue of a special breed of people; everyone should get the opportunity to engage in the creative mode.

A few years ago, I interviewed a couple who operated a high-stress marketing company. With a keen awareness of the threat of burnout in their creative-thinking environment, the wife prepared a "revival room" where employees could get some "me" time during the workday. They could visit the revival room any time for meditation, prayer, a nap, silent contemplation, or just to space out for a while. The leading couple of this company found that this room increased the creative input and output of employees.

- Trust. The reality of today's workplace demonstrates that there is still a great lack of trust in workforce members. It may be that some workplaces require a greater level of employee scrutiny, but companies such as Google, Atlassian, and the SAS Institute have proven the astounding effects of allowing employees time for themselves and investing trust in them.

A common denominator in all of the above is broad inclusion and our general perception of the corporation; no effort toward more inclusion and creative output will succeed when there are silos in the organization and some employee groups sense that some are treated in a more privileged way than others. Similarly, no effort to establish a creatively contributing workforce will pay off when we hold a negative perspective of our company's reputation, strategies toward stakeholders, and distribution of profits. The time that employees were ignorant about these strategic matters is history. Today's employee is well-educated, harbors a healthy dose of intellectual curiosity, and has access to many resources. Smart managers keep that in mind.

- Fit. If we hate our jobs, we only will be creative in finding ways to avoid them. If we love what we do, however, we are more likely to bring creativity to our work. It is critical, therefore, to have the right fit between an employee and his/her work. Feeling that our work matters, that we are appreciated, and that there is a proper fit between our talents and our work is crucial for releasing our creative juices.
- Communication. In work environments where there are good communication flows, we feel more involved. When we are treated as if we matter, when we feel valued, and when we find that there are ample ways to convey opinions and ideas, most of us will feel encouraged to become engaged. Communication, therefore, is a very important aspect in making or breaking creativity levels in contemporary workplaces, where knowledge sharing is a critical foundation for creative performance. Carla O'Dell and Cindy Hubert

(2011) emphasize that a knowledge-sharing culture will result in increased collaboration, faster yet more thorough output, and mutual recognition.

Connecting Creativity and Innovation

All creative thoughts may not lead to innovation. In their 2012 article about the correlation between creativity and innovation, Ozge Çokpekin and Mette Knudsen confirm that creativity does not necessarily lead to innovation; we can only make creativity useful if we know what type of innovation we aim to achieve. In addition, they state that the organization also should demonstrate certain characteristics that will support this relationship, such as being aware of mental models; facilitating review of issues through multiple frames; and establishing a trustful environment where communication, recognition, and motivation are cultivated.

It seems safe to assert that a workforce consisting of creative thinkers, who feel encouraged to share their insights because they receive space and are trusted, will find the path for innovation unlocked. This clarifies the need for organizations to provide a supportive climate, as a means of driving innovation and improving business performance.

References

Bolman, L. G., & Deal, T. E. (2008). *Reframing Organizations: Artistry, Choice, and Leadership* (4th ed.). John Wiley & Sons, Inc., Hoboken, NJ.

Çokpekin, O., & Knudsen, M. P. (2012). Does organizing for creativity really lead to innovation? *Creativity and Innovation Management, 21*(3), pp. 304–314.

Csíkszentmihályi, M. (2008). *Flow: The Psychology of Optimal Experience.* Harper Perennial Modem Classics, New York, NY.

de Bono, E. (1988). Serious creativity. *The Journal for Quality and Participation, 18*(5), p. 12.

Dickson, J. V. (2003). Killing creativity: How unspoken sentiments affect workplace creativity. *The Journal for Quality and Participation, 26*(2), p. 40.

Marques, J., Dhiman, S., & King, R. (2007). *Spirituality in the Workplace: What It Is, Why It Matters, How to Make It Work for You.* Personhood Press, Fawnskin, CA.

O'Dell, C., & Hubert, C. (2011). Building a knowledge-sharing culture. *The Journal for Quality and Participation, 34*(2), pp. 22–26.

Perakis, E. (2011). How to grow creativity and innovation in your company. *Global Focus, 5*, pp. 32–35.

Peters, T. (1999). *The Brand You 50: Or: Fifty Ways to Transform Yourself From an "Employee" Into a Brand That Shouts Distinction, Commitment, and Passion!* Alfred A. Knopf, Inc, New York, NY.

Robinson, C. (2010). The keys to turbo-charging intrinsic motivation. *The Journal for Quality and Participation, 33*(3), pp. 4–8.

Senge, P. M. (2006). *The Fifth Discipline: the Art & Practice of the Learning Organization.* Doubleday, New York, NY.

39

THAT SOCIAL ASPECT

Many people often say that working in business is diehard. That may be true in some ways. Yet, working in other environments has similar challenges. Academia, nonprofit, governmental—all work environments have one important thing in common: interaction of people with each other in different settings. Some of those people are coworkers, others are customers or clients, yet others suppliers, and then you have some others who may work in competitive camps. The overarching aspect in all of this is that they are stakeholders, and as such we are socializing with them. We socialize at different levels and on a continuous basis, and the types of conversations we have depended on where the parties stand in the connection scheme. This means that our connection often requires alertness in what we say, how, and when. It's an evolutionary and revolutionary process. Evolutionary, because relationships evolve based on changing positions and social settings, and revolutionary, because we all have to redefine our position based on new developments.

In the midst of all this revolutionary thinking and acting, we can still be graceful and candid in social interactions. And the attitude of elegance and sincerity can be performed toward partners, subordinates, suppliers, and competitors alike! There has never been a rule that excluded correct behavior from being a good stakeholder. Actually, you can only perform well in any environment if you take a graceful approach seriously in all your actions.

According to the belief system of the Navajo, there are two sides to every aspect of life, and one cannot be without the other: for example, dark needs light and good needs bad. This train of thought could be extended to private as well as professional issues, and we can conclude that revolution readiness needs gracefulness, change alertness needs flexibility, and lasting success needs honesty. Think about it: how could you possibly be able to perform excellently in the long run without creating solid room for serene harmony in your life? Isn't this more or less what the idea behind our eternal quest for balance? The strongest leaders and the most renowned gurus never seem to miss an opportunity to stress the importance of balance: making sure that all relevant areas in our lives are covered and that, hence, physical wellness gets as much attention as mental health.

Stephen R. Covey (1994) mentions the balance issue time and again in his *The 7 Habits of Highly Effective People: Powerful Lessons in Personal Change*. One example is the time-management lecture, in which he encourages us to try to remain in quadrant 2, where matters are important, but not urgent (yet), and prevent them from becoming quadrant 1 issues, where they are important and urgent, and thus, stressful! Covey explains that doing things when there is still enough time protects us from getting stressed out, while it enables us at the same time to create room for performing the physical activities needed to stay in good health. He emphasizes this once more when introducing the seventh habit, sharpening the saw, in which he encourages his audience to create time for relaxation, breathing, and whatever is needed to regain strength and fresh perceptions.

So, what is it that can enhance gracefulness in our social interactions? How about this incomplete list of advice:

- Be friendly and accessible. Even to competitors, salespeople, and the ones that are miles underneath you on the social ladder. It pays off when you're on your way back.
- Keep yourself down to earth. Mingle with regular people on a frequent basis. Go to a movie, dine in an inexpensive restaurant, take a stroll on the beach. There are countless ways to meet people who—perhaps unintentionally—will keep you focused on who you really are.
- Give. Wealth is not the only reason to make gestures, and money is not the only thing you can give! Contribute your knowledge, your time, your efforts, or your connections to others that need a boost. You have been there. Now it's your turn to do something, even if you think there was no one who helped you to get where you are now.
- Consider the reasons. People never act without a motive, yet, sometimes it takes time to find out what drives them in certain directions. But it may be worth your while. So, find out why your employees, suppliers, competitors, or other constituents in the business field do what they do. And never assume that they were ill-intended from the very start. Seek to understand.
- Don't underestimate the power of MBWA (Management by Walking Around). It is the perfect way to communicate with people, whom you otherwise never would have talked to. It enhances your chances of being updated on their interests, their discontents, on the latest shoo-shoo out there (yes, many strategic decisions have come forth from those!) And, believe it or not, it creates a tremendous amount of goodwill born out of the recognition you

gave; an aspect that might turn out to be helpful when tides turn and you will need votes to remain where you thought you belonged!

- Treat competitors as colleagues rather than enemies. No one knows what tomorrow brings: it may be a situation where you will need their support. A competitor is in the first place a fellow human being.
- Prevent neglect of the ones in your private life. They are the wind beneath your wings, but while you fly, you may not realize that well enough. Yet, now that it is spelled out here for you, you can start planning on spending considerable time with family, friends, sport mates, and other loved ones. And don't underestimate the good influence being a family-oriented person has on your business reputation?

You just read 7 of the 1,001 habits of graceful professionals. Without a doubt you could come up with a number of similar approaches. The basic advice is, to never forget yourself, and to be graceful inside and outside of the work arena.

Reference

Covey, S. R. (1994). *The 7 Habits of Highly Effective People: Powerful Lessons in Personal Change*. DC Books, New York, NY.

40

ON GIVING BACK

It's easier to take than to give. It's nobler to give than to take. The thrill of taking lasts a day. The thrill of giving lasts a lifetime.

–Joan Marques

Every day brings us numerous opportunities to be a hero. Not necessarily the kind that will be profiled in the newspaper or on television, and not the kind that will get you a medal of honor or any other special recognition from the government, but the kind that leaves a warm feeling inside, and that positively contributes to the scale of good versus evil.

Being an everyday hero is a noble act of giving back to the universe, and silently saying "thank you" for all the blessings you received. True: it won't add any dollars to your wallet or bank account, but it surely will add value to your very core.

Doing something good can be as miniscule as placing a rain worm that lost its way, and will dry out on the sidewalk, back onto the wet soil, so that it has a chance to survive; or picking up that shirt that desolately lies on the floor in the store where you happen to shop. Or making sure that the restroom you used is left in decent state for the next person, even if no one will penalize you if you don't. Or closing the tap when you brush your teeth, and only open it again to rinse your mouth, even if you don't pay the water bill. Or forgiving someone for something they did to you. Or granting someone the right of way, even if you don't have to.

Doing something good is a spiritual act. It has nothing to do with your heritage, culture, religion, age, gender, ethnicity, or political beliefs, but everything with making the world a better place, one small heroic act at a time.

Here are seven reasons why you should do something good today:

1. It doesn't take anything away from you. Okay, it may cost you a moment or two, but the act itself is usually small, quick, and almost effortless.
2. You have a chance to make another living being happy. You may not always detect a smile on the face of the one who benefits from your kindness, but your heart will confirm that you did the right thing.
3. The universe takes copious notes. No good deed goes unrecognized, and something good will be returned to you at an unexpected moment in an unexpected way.
4. A small act of virtuousness will make you feel better about the world and yourself. It will reassure you that there is still good in this world because you just confirmed that with your own action.
5. It is just the right thing to do. Even if you don't believe in any of the points mentioned previously, it is hard to convince yourself that doing something good would be a bad thing. Some of you may ask, "How do I know that I am actually doing something good?" The answer: just listen to your gut feeling: in most cases, you know intuitively if what you do is the right thing or not.
6. The more you engage in acts of daily heroism, the greater the balance of virtuousness in our collective human behavior becomes. This is your chance to deliver a contribution in a world where so many of us feel so powerless: here's where you make a difference, and the more differences you make, the more our collective heroic barometer will rise.
7. Regularly engaging in daily heroic acts will not escape the attention of others. While you may not receive anything else, you will receive gratitude, and with that, well-wishes. You may inspire others to become everyday heroes as well! You may even become a role model to some!

Doing something good can be addictive because it feels so good. Once you have experienced that warm feeling inside, you may want to trigger it again, and again. Engaging in everyday heroism is a wonderful addiction. Perhaps the only wonderful addiction there is. Try it. You'll like it!

41

THE SPIRITUAL SIDE

I'M NOT SURE . . .

It seems that most people
Need to hear some kind of sound
Which means that, in most places,
There's no quietude to be found

In absence of media, phone or friend,
Many prefer to hear their own voice
Consumed by this ceaseless craving
For any kind of conceivable noise

Perhaps silence is now taboo
This jewel of a substance so fine
This soothing mental blanket
Frail sanctuary—sacred shrine

Oasis of listening to thoughts
Honoring the breath given at birth
Reacquainting with forgotten senses
And savoring the stillness of Earth

Why is silence so hard to find?
Are most thoughts too hard to endure?

> Why do people ignore their mind?
> I'm at a loss here . . . I'm not sure.
>
> ~ *Joan Marques*

Like a moving windmill, our perceptions change. Stability only lasts for a while, and depending on the size of the project or the intensity of the emotion at hand, this "while" may last shorter or longer. But "a while" it will be anyway, for even the most valuable experiences today may seem meaningless tomorrow through changes in perceptions, whether generated by external developments or not.

That's the change we go through: call it spiritual evolution, mental growth, or just human transformation. A love that we once cherished with the deepest care may gradually transform into a gutless camaraderie that could be discarded without much regret. A corporate vision we proudly developed and shared barely a decade ago may seem hollow and unbefitting in today's reality. A passion we once had toward a desirable goal may have imperceptibly altered, either into a dreadful mission or into an entirely different vision.

Changes within are often stimulated by changes around. But spiritual evolution is a factor we should not underestimate in the process. Sometimes it may happen that all factors remain the same, and yet our feelings or perceptions change.

The hardest part of this fact is that we may find ourselves refusing to admit it because we dread being perceived as inconsistent, unreliable, or weak. Thus, for the sake of perceived stability, dependability, and strength, we hold on to dreams, visions, and relationships that lost their value to us, yet got trapped in, simply because we once enthusiastically embarked upon them.

However, if you care to take a few steps back and attempt to view this "change" phenomenon from a distance, you may find that the entire structure of our current social system is actually restrictive to our natural human mentality: By engaging in legal agreements of any other kind, personally or professionally, we directly contradict the natural change process that we, ever-evolving human beings, are prone to.

That being said, it is also true that some sort of structure is inevitable, and that organization and lawful confirmation of the promises we make and the responsibilities we take is a necessity, as a world of extravagance would probably lead to insurmountable problems, to a much higher degree than the ones we currently cope with. Yet: the very fact that lawful confirmation is a necessity does not make it much easier to digest.

Although in corporate and societal matters change is not favored, it is dealt with in one way or another: corporations alter their strategies and their production lines when they find that the old ways are not in demand anymore. This may take shorter or longer, depending on the level of awareness and flexibility from the corporation's leaders, and the nature and size of the organization in total.

But personal change may be a harder one to deal with, especially if it is not initiated by external factors, but rather by inner evolution. How do you tell someone who once was your world that you don't really care anymore, even though nothing significant has changed? How do you explain the wear and tear on your desire, which caused you to lose interest? How do you, thus, sell the natural process of change within one changing human being to another in a society that has taught us that such is bad?

The answer to this is still up there somewhere. You can try using superb communication skills, and you may even be able to make it acceptable to the other party. But how about your own emotional state? Ever tried to understand this evolution within yourself? Or are you just allowing it to come over you without too much brain- or heart trouble? If you can do that, you have either settled for acceptance of the incomprehensible, like the majority of religious followers, or you have managed to comprehend something many others are still struggling with. And in the latter case: be our mentor!

42

A DASH OF HUMOR

Here's a lighthearted story to underscore that we should not take ourselves too seriously at all times.

A misunderstood genius was walking on a plain not far from a great metropolitan city, at 3 pm while the sun was high in the sky, and the earth was splitting from drought. He was there because he needed some time to contemplate in a quiet environment. However; his troubled state of mind was not cooperating too well with his desire to generate some fruitful ideas.

He kicked a single cactus that just eyed a little too bouncy and bubbly for his antagonistic mood. "The nerve of this plant to stand there so vivacious in such sizzling sun. It should be against the law!" he grumbled. But the cactus stung him right through his canvas shoe, and the misunderstood genius uttered a cry from pain.

While rubbing the sore toes of his right foot with his left hand, the misunderstood genius saw a middle-aged woman in a light khaki outfit observing him with a gaze that hovered between amusement and mild aggravation.

"Silly man," the woman said, "You should have known how the cactus would respond to your foolish deed."

"Cactuses can't talk, woman, and I just didn't kick it hard enough, I guess."

"Oh you kicked hard alright," replied the woman, "But the cactus was not going to let you get away with your unfounded aggression. Everything has a message for you, don't you know? The cactus just told you that you should never hurt or insult others without expecting the same in return. So, in fact the cactus just maintained the golden rule: Don't do unto others what you don't want to be done unto yourself. But tell me, why are you actually so upset today?"

"Well, not that it's any of your business, but my life has not been running very smoothly lately," answered the misunderstood genius. "I just got laid off from my job as a promising engineer because some character at the other end of the world offered my company similar service for half the hourly rate. And that happened just while I was well on my way to developing a new device at home: a device that would cut the production costs for my company in half, while shortening the delivery time with 35%. But I guess it just took a little too long, and the extent of my luck was just a little too short to achieve my goal before they let me go."

"So, what does it take for you to finish the development of this new device on your own and sell it to either the company you recently worked for, or another?"

"Hmmm . . . I hadn't thought about that. Actually, it wouldn't take too much additional effort, since the blueprint is almost ready." The misunderstood genius was actually starting to smile again. His energy noticeably increased, while a gleam replaced the dimness that had been in his eyes just a moment ago. "In fact, I am pretty sure that I will get an opportunity to present my plan if it is well constructed and comprehensive enough. They never ignore proposals that warrant great potential return on investment and efficiency increase. And I believe that the very fact that I am providing the company that recently let me go with this primer instead of vindictively offering it to their main competitor, may create a different dimension in our relationship."

"Wise thinking!" replied the woman, "You are not repaying good with evil. Your genius is on the rise!"

Just as sudden as the woman had appeared she gone was again. But the misunderstood genius felt reenergized, hurried home, finished the blueprint, settled his patent and copyright issues, and made an appointment with the top management of the company he had been working for during the preceding four years. Within three weeks he gave a spectacular presentation, and became a very prestigious consultant for the company, making ten times more money than he used to as an employee.

But the financial prosperity was not the most important improvement in the genius' life. Even more essential to him was the dignity that he regained by learning to perceive himself as an equal partner with the company he was once just working for. This newly gained dignity spawned tremendous inspiration within the genius, and he went on to develop multiple sophisticated devices, not only for the company he was now advising but also for others in- and outside the industry where he used to work.

His quest to develop elicited a new curiosity within him, and he started approaching organizations far outside the borders of his country as well.

One day, while he was daydreaming in his small, but state-of-the-art workplace that he had built annex to his house, the middle-aged woman in khaki reappeared. "Congratulations, my friend, you did it!" she said smilingly. "Now let's see, what have you gained in the past months? You became an independent worker: your own boss, and you feel good about this responsibility. In fact, you feel so good about it that your creative spirit has been triggered and has flourished since then. You have established connections with companies in countries located in at least three continents of the world. You are about to do some nice traveling in the near future, and will make yourself familiar with the world 'out there'." Your database of connections looks good: it has at least 17 new names in it. You became multifaceted. You see yourself as an organization nowadays, and not as the victimized worker you used to be. Heck, you have even been contemplating to write a technical guide for your line of expertise! You simply took the challenge that was placed on your path by that "overseas character that stole your job," and transformed it into an opportunity for yourself. You learned from his example, and really got yourself going! And throughout this entire mental crash course you took, you also learned about self-respect, respect for others, the essence of familiarity with various cultures, and the overall importance of being proactive. But do you know the main message that life conferred to you in the past months?

The genius didn't even have to think about that one: "I have learned that there is a misunderstood genius in all of us, and that we have a choice: We can either dwell on the aggravation of being neglected or misunderstood, and make the world an increasingly worse place for ourselves and all others around us, or we can change our attitude and find other ways to earn recognition while also understanding that there will be a time we'll see the humor of any situation we encounter. The secret lies in searching, persevering, and daring."

The woman in khaki winked and disappeared, and the genius woke up from his refreshing afternoon nap.

43

GIVE YOUR ALL AND LET GO

HOW BLESSINGS ARE EARNED

Give the gift of love, because the world needs it
Give the gift of peace: you'll find it in your heart
Give the gift of support, because someone deserves it
Give the gift of knowledge, because you're smart

Give the gift of listening: you can, because you care
Give the gift of affection, as it warms all around
Give the gift of good thoughts, even if no one sees them
Give the gift of sharing: it's a hard one to be found

Give the gift of truth: it's almost wiped out today
Give the gift of trust, and you'll find it is returned
Give the gift of goodwill, as a dedicated human
Give the gift of giving: it's how blessings are earned

~ Joan Marques

If there has ever been a power that comes suspiciously close to an art, it is "letting go." In an earlier section of this book (Hurt and Aversion), the art of letting go was already addressed, so this section will be brief and will start with a story.

I heard this story in India during a Vipassana meditation course. Vipassana meditation aims at becoming enlightened through the understanding that nothing is permanent, so nothing is worth clinging to. The story is about two brothers living and working on a farm with their father. Life was well, and everything went its merry way until one day the father died.

The two sons did what they had to do, and after the funeral, decided to immediately clean up their beloved father's cabinet. They found a little box with two rings: one very expensive golden ring with diamonds, obviously a very exquisite piece of art, and a simple silver ring with no special features.

The oldest brother, always a demanding and dissatisfied one, quickly claimed the expensive ring, telling his younger brother that their father would have probably wanted it this way, since he was the oldest son, and would keep it as a family piece to be inherited later by his oldest son.

The younger brother, always a calm and peaceful one, agreed and simply took the silver ring. Life continued its normal way, and one evening the young brother was sitting on the front porch, enjoying the evening. His eyes fell on the silver ring he was now always wearing. He wondered again why his father would have kept such a simple, insignificant-looking ring . . . He pulled it off his finger and held it against the light. That's when he found out that something was engraved in the ring. As he looked better, he could read the words, "This too shall pass." The young man smiled and understood instantly why his father had kept this simple ring so dearly.

This message is strong and has the ability to bring you back to earth immediately. If you feel invincible due to a strike of luck, this statement could calm you down, realizing that everything is temporary. Similarly, if you feel down and out due to a series of mishaps, this statement could make you feel better, as you will understand that the negative spiral will end in the near future.

Mastering the power to let go involves self-respect, resilience, broadmindedness, acceptance, confidence, decisiveness, responsibility, and personality. This incomplete enumeration may clarify why letting go is not easy: Not in business, and certainly not in your private life. A closer look at the aforementioned required abilities to obtain the power of letting go may give insight in the reasons why these skills are so necessary to make "letting go" work.

Self-respect should, in this case, be perceived with consideration of Shakespeare's words, "This above all; to thine own self be true." Self-respect is therefore needed for the realization that the release you are about to execute is best for your feelings toward yourself.

Resilience is as important as Abraham Lincoln described it when he told the following tale, "It is said an eastern monarch once charged his wise men to invent a sentence, to be ever in view, and which should be true and appropriate in all times and situations. They presented him with the words, 'And this, too, shall pass away'. How much it expresses! How chastening in the hour of pride! How consoling in the depths of affliction!" (Lincoln, ND). Resilience is, hence, crucial to be able to continue after the release has taken place.

Broadmindedness is required, in order to see the big picture of the overall advantage and the long-term benefit that this act will bring. However, remember too, that broadmindedness enables you to see both sides of a problem, but you may not necessarily see the solution.

Acceptance is in place here, because you will not only have to live with yourself after making and executing your decision, but you will also have to live without the object or person that you released. Release represents a change—and the only way we can successfully change anything is to first accept it.

Confidence is also necessary; because you want to be sure that your decision is one you fully support. For that reason, "Speak what you think today in words as hard as cannon-balls and to-morrow speak what to-morrow thinks in hard words again, though it contradicts everything you said to-day" (Emerson, ND). Only when you are sure of what you are doing, and only if you are ready to accept all the consequences, should you do it.

Decisiveness speaks for itself in this list of qualities: if you are unable to make bold decisions, you will get stuck with unwanted and unnecessary burdens in your life. Anything is better than just hanging in there, for "indecision is like a stepchild: if he does not wash his hands, he is called dirty, if he does, he is wasting water" (African Proverb, ND).

Responsibility is the driver you need, in order to know why you are releasing this particular person, strategy, company, or object, because you don't want this situation to turn into a disaster for any party—the least yourself. It is also the unlimited strength you will have to rely on after the release is factual. Remember that "responsibility walks hand in hand with capacity and power" (Holland, J. G., ND).

Personality, finally, is the overall skill you need in working up the strength to make decisions, bounce back, move on, accept consequences, and mature even further after each release. It is a skill that develops slowly. Actually, "personality is born out of pain. It is the fire shut up in the flint." (Yeats, J. B., ND).

Letting go is not funny. Nowhere. Never. Think of the manager that has to fire a number of his coworkers in the downsizing process of a company, while he knows that all these people have families who depend on their income. Think about the CEO that has to put off a merger, which he knows would have been beneficial to the company, because there are other issues that make it strategically imprudent to be executed at this moment. Think about the man who has to allow the vet to put his beloved pet to sleep forever, because it has been incurably ill for some time now, knowing how sorely he will miss it. Think about the woman who needs to let go of the man she dearly loves, for whatever reason that may be.

The real positive outcome of letting go is, that we mature, every time we have to practice it. It is usually accompanied by a variety of pains: growing pains. But in the end, it may be worthwhile. Or at least one should hope so.

References

African Proverb. (ND). Innocent is like a stepchild . . . *Quotes.net*. Retrieved from www.quotes.net/quote/42454.

Emerson, R. W. (ND). Else if you would be a man . . . *Goodreads.com*. Retrieved from www.goodreads.com/quotes/267010-else-if-you-would-be-a-man-speak-what-you.

Holland, J. G. (ND). Responsibility walks hand in hand . . . *Brainyquote.com*. Retrieved from www.brainyquote.com/quotes/josiah_gilbert_holland_152655.

Lincoln, A. (ND). It is said . . . *Goodreads.com*. Retrieved from www.goodreads.com/quotes/26401-it-is-said-an-eastern-monarch-once-charged-his-wise.

Yeats, J. B. (ND). Personality is born out of pain . . . *Goodreads.com*. Retrieved from www.goodreads.com/quotes/99148-personality-is-born-out-of-pain-it-is-the-fire.

44

STOP COMPARING!

Comparing is something we all do at times, only to realize afterward that it only jumbles up our peace of mind. Comparing is a risky practice because you never know the full story behind others' circumstances, so it is actually never a fair practice—neither to yourself, not to others.

Jiddu Krishnamurti, a great philosopher, once admitted that he only obtained his calm demeanor when he stopped comparing. In an interview, taking from him one year before he passed away, in 1985, he even likened the act of comparing to violence. Wise and insightful as he was, he explained that the habit of comparing is taught to us from childhood on (Krishnamurti, 1985). Mothers who, without bad intentions, encourage their children to do better than others. Siblings who compete in looks and performance. Teens who compare their outfits to those from their classmates. He even warns for the mindset of "if I do this, then . . .," because it instigates thoughts of rewards or punishments, which is yet another form of comparing.

And yet, comparison is such an embedded part of human performance. It compels toward excellence, and even in corporate settings, there is an eternal cycle of comparing, which we call benchmarking.

Nonetheless, Krishnamurti makes a lot of sense: comparing is a form of violence, primarily to ourselves because it pushes us to do things we might otherwise not even consider doing. It robs us from our peace of mind and presses us toward ever-higher levels of performance.

Comparing is sometimes also a shortcut toward action, when a person runs out of ideas and options, which could be rekindled by peeking what others do. After all, mental paralysis is a terrible phenomenon to deal with, every time it shows up. Business people—like no other—know the cost of indecisiveness. The statement "Time is money" was definitely not invented by the first the best poet. It doesn't even sound poetic! But it is also a truism in the world of business performance.

With indecisiveness we use up time that could be valuable in obtaining a competitive advantage toward our rivals. However—the risk of making the wrong decision is always lurking behind every corner of strategy street, and so—being the ordinary creatures with little or no psychic gifts that most of us are—we need to weigh our chances and base our decisions on some sort of information or hunch on possible outcomes. Here's where business people usually fall into the pattern of following statistical trends, or relying on economic and financial advisors, who basically do the same: they compare with others. The more daring ones intermittently also rely on their intuition. If, then, the decision turns out to be wrong they can always console themselves by reasoning that at least it was an informed and calculated mistake.

And then there is the other side of comparing, whereby we label others almost at first sight. Given the statistically proven fact that we are all guilty—to some extent—of branding others with a rapidly working mind, during the first 5 to 20 seconds that we see them, we should be concerned about and think on this. Keeping an open mind is a wonderful piece of advice, but how does it tie into our habit of labeling at first sight, and our tendency to compare?

An open mind indicates that we should eliminate our prejudices, and only form careful conclusions after thorough exposure to the subject of our attention. It also indicates that we withhold ourselves from making the vulgar mistake of letting the eye see only what the mind is prepared to comprehend. One question that may arise is, should we leave enough space for adjustments to a carefully developed mental picture (as opposed to a first glance label), since all living creatures are constant subject to change.

The point of maintaining an open mind may best be illustrated by holding a psychological mirror in front of ourselves, while asking, don't we realize that we are continuously changing? That every new experience influences our thinking and reactions from that moment on? That we are all subject to mood swings and a natural process of maturing—one faster than the other—And—perhaps most shockingly—that some of us may never really get to know ourselves? Whether you think that sounds ridiculous or not, many great thinkers have brought it up before, like Goethe, who stated, " 'Know thyself?' If I knew myself, I'd run away." If we understand all of the above about ourselves, it should not be hard to conclude that others may also have been—and are still—going through their share of changes.

It may require some mental digging, but try to remember a time when you got disappointed in someone whom you initially thought the world of—simply because of something he or she said, did, or lacked to say or do? Or, on a positive note: think of the person that pleasantly surprised after a rather weak and dull first impression!

Whether the aforementioned situations have actually occurred in your life or not, they're not unthinkable. The mere fact that "surprise" is an existing word in our vocabulary should be a major indication to us that we should allow surprises to happen, and the best way we can do so is to work on our tendency to make quick comparisons, followed by hasty judgments.

An open mind is a powerful tool that may be hard to obtain, given the fact that we all grow up with certain biases, cultural baggage, and deeply rooted beliefs. Yet, the more our spirit matures, the greater our mind's potential becomes—and the more room will be created for receptiveness. And when we think of the peace that can be part of our lives when we stop comparing, we may very well get tempted to do just that.

Reference

Krishnamurti, J. (1985). Isn't comparing a form of violence? *JKrishnamurti.org*. Retrieved from https://jkrishnamurti.org/content/isnt-comparison-form-violence.

45

APPRECIATE YOURSELF

The things you learn are but vehicles serving to transport you toward further knowledge and awareness. You can therefore not necessarily cling to the things you learn, because they may become obsolete through changes in time and circumstances.

As a logical consequence of this, you should not be afraid to release thoughts, contacts, and perspectives, no matter how valuable they seemed at one time. For, responsibly releasing old thoughts, contacts, and perspectives is a way to enhance your receptivity toward new, more rewarding ones in current times.

People and things serve a purpose in your life, as do you in theirs. However, when it is time to move on, you should do so without regret but with gratitude for the contribution these people and things made to your growth and with hope that you may have done the same to theirs.

The main purpose of your being is to grow: to reach a higher plane of insight, not just in business matters or in intellectual regards, but in emotional areas as well.

And reaching a higher plane of insight is a fascinating journey, because not all of us need the same vehicles or routes of learning to get there. And yet, we may all arrive at this higher plane. But it is important to keep in mind that, as many people there are reaching a particular level of insight, as many roads and vehicles may have led them there. Some may have achieved their growth predominantly through formal education: absorbing lectures and reading books; others through street smartness: meeting people and seeing things; yet others through a combination of both, or through less traditional journeys: abstinence, meditation, and self-mentoring, for instance.

So, can you say, then, that one vehicle, meaning one method to reach a higher plane, is more valuable than another? Of course not! Therefore, should you get blinded by one's titles, ranges, prefixes, suffixes, or the absolute lack thereof? Of course not! More importantly: should you judge one's knowledge on basis of his or her background, experiences, ethnicity, culture, religion, or sex? Of course not! And yet: look around you. Reflect on your own life or the lives of the ones you know: review your and their careers and try to evaluate how many times this very superficial way of judging has either positively or negatively influenced the course of those careers.

How beautiful would it be if people could meet at a certain level of insight and exchange with each other the roads they traveled and the vehicles they used to get there? How enriching would it be for them, as well as for those who succeed them! For these successors may later take note of the records of this shared knowledge, and thus learn about the abundance of vehicles available to reach an elevated level of insight, and perhaps, at that time, add some new ones to the list.

It is all about growth: about reaching a higher plane; about insight; about contentment and, thus, about understanding. You can be a leader of a global corporation or a political organization, determining the fates of thousands with a snap of your fingers, or you can be a homemaker, determining what to present your loved ones for dinner tonight; you can be an intellectual, determining how to best transmit your lectures to your students tomorrow, or you can be an average worker in a small, midsize or large workplace determining how to survive between now and your next paycheck; you can be an entrepreneur, searching for the fastest way of earning recognition and achieving growth for your venture, or you can be a convinced loner, determining not to follow any direction but your own.

Regardless of who you are: growth is achievable, and vehicles for growth are available. Learning is not limited to the formal settings, no matter how persuasively society will try to convince you about that. Learning can happen everywhere, but you should see it merely as a vehicle to get to a higher plane: to grow. Because that is the purpose of life.

46

THE TEACHERS IN YOUR LIFE

One perspective that can make a lot of your experiences worthwhile is to see everything and everyone as a teacher. People, animals, experiences, they all entail valuable lessons that can help us make better decisions in the future.

Every day is a teacher in its own right as well. And every day is unique in its own way. And like formal teachers in class settings, some days come across better than others. Those are the ones where the traffic lights all seem to jump on green when you get near, when people are smiling, and when things seem to go well in every area. But then there are those days where you feel like shooting everything and everybody: nothing seems to fit, no one seems to cooperate, and everything seems to be set against you. We've all been there.

It is unfortunate, though, that we often neglect the fact that the latter described days are as natural a part of life as the first and equally valuable teachers in the wholeness of our lives. And yet, many cultures, religions, and wise individuals have tried to teach it to us during many centuries: everything needs to be balanced out. There cannot be good without bad, there cannot be happy without sad; there cannot be dark without light, and there cannot be day without night.

All I'm trying to say here is that the "bad" days, just like other "bad" things that overcome us, are equally valuable teachers to us as the good ones. We just don't notice their purpose at the time that they're happening to us. Sometimes blessings manifest themselves disguised as curses. It's only later that we realize why we had to go through the pain of a dreadful experience. Oftentimes it turns out to be because there was something much better for us in store.

And about those bad days: Although we may not always see their purpose right away, we can still do something constructive with them. We can review them at their end, and mentally list the lessons we learned from what happened within them. We can also modify the retrospective emotions toward those days by formulating our evaluations in a positive way. We can, for instance, develop a standard list of affirmative focus points for every day's end.

Here's an example of such a list:

- Who was the nicest person I met today, and what did he or she do that stood out compared to the rest?
- What was the most unique action I undertook today, and why did I do it?
- What was the most beautiful thing I encountered today, and what was it that alerted me on its beauty?
- What was the strongest statement I heard today, and what did I find so exceptional about it?
- What was the most valuable act I executed today, and why do I consider it important?
- What was the most pleasant thing I did today, and why did I enjoy it that much?

The list can be shorter or longer, and, of course, entirely different in formulation, depending on what you want to focus on. But once you have your positive attention points listed it is easy to subsequently formulate the lessons you learned from those points, and you can start valuing the teachers that presented you those lessons.

47

EVERYTHING HAS A PURPOSE

The most rewarding purpose you can have is one that will benefit others as well.

There is no time when more people determine their future purpose than around the dawning of a new year, whether that is a calendar year, or a year in a person's lifetime. It's at these moments that we look back at the past 12 months with mixed emotions. Some of us are more satisfied than others. However, those of us who have a nagging feeling of insufficient accomplishment should consider that every achievement requires input and collaboration from various factors. So, you can't possibly take all the blame for things that went wrong.

At the times when we contemplate about our life, we try to formulate our intentions, and therefore our purpose. Business executives may plan for ways to make a strategic breakthrough; lonely people may pray for the final encounter with their soul mate; the ones that experience financial hardship may hope for the long-awaited reward for their hard work; and creative spirits may lay out their tactics for earning the recognition they consider to deserve.

Some of us announce our intentions with much fanfare, while others prefer to keep their objectives to themselves. Those are probably the ones that believe that too much talking about an issue will jinx the whole thing and ultimately lead to nothing. And maybe there is some truth to their thinking: the more people you inform about your plans, the more negative energy may be released in the environment by their envy, whether vented consciously or unconsciously.

Yet, regardless if you're one of the silent purpose formulators, or whether you prefer a more boisterous approach, you may consider honoring this crucial mindset: make sure that your purpose will not deliberately be harmful to any living being in particular. In business settings, this may be a little more difficult than in others, because competition is a tough phenomenon that unfortunately often leads to winners and losers. However, as long as personal vendetta is kept out of the picture, there is a much better chance of succeeding.

Purposes are interesting things: we make them with our own progress in mind. And that's not a bad thing at all. There are many schools of thought that believe that everyone is ultimately an egoist. Seen from that perspective, even the noblest seeming act is performed from an egoistic point of view, if only to feel better about oneself. And yes, we may unintentionally bring pain and damage to others with our purpose, but, like the German philosopher Emmanuel Kant believed, it's not the outcome that matters as much as the intention. Elaborating on Kant's theory this can be interpreted as follows: "If your intention is good, a disastrous outcome is forgivable. However, if your intention was bad from the start, even a positive outcome will know no blessing or fortitude."

Also, try to formulate your purpose in such a way that as many others as possible can benefit from it. It feels so much better if you know that what you achieve will not only make a positive difference in your life, but in the life of at least one other person as well. This is how an extrinsic reward generates an intrinsic fulfillment at the same time.

And while we're at it, here are some points to ponder as you reflect on your purpose from here onward:

- Regardless of your religious convictions, culture, status, or descend: Always try to make a gesture toward the ones you meet. Live. And let live. For You Can't Take It With You . . .
- When confronted with a problem: don't get paranoid, but analyze the gist of it, and tackle it systematically. Problems are the forebears of change, and change is inevitable.
- Success is the one thing you work for after having defined it yourself. Obtaining it will depend on your own input, the choices you make, and the degree to which you want to stretch yourself.
- Don't ever take anything for granted, no matter how safe and secure it may seem. The day that you will have to reapply your flexibility and adaptation to change may be nearer than you think!
- Fear is definitely the most important reason why people cease to undertake certain actions. Yet, fear should be seen in its right proportions and its legitimate occurrence. Sometimes people will discourage you to execute a marvelous plan not out of fear but out of jealousy or conflicting personal agendas! It's up to you to see these possible reasons in their right perspective and—more importantly—to prevent them from dispiriting you.
- Life is a bag full of surprises, presented to each of us, every day again. Some surprises taste sweet, but most of them have a bitter foretaste. It is up to us, then, to adapt our taste buds to these new challenges, and unleash our positive imagination and our sense of humor on them, so that we will be able to detect the sweetness that is hidden behind the initial gall.

- We all perceive life through glasses that were colored by our education, ethnicity, culture, gender, age, personal convictions, political ideologies, religion, and wealth. Our colored glasses determine how we choose to perceive the things that happen to us, faultlessly guiding us toward the option that is least detrimental to our self-perception and our self-esteem.
- We should always attempt to determine when to measure with different standards and when to measure with only one. People are equal: they, therefore, deserve equal treatment and equal chances. However: the way to approach an individual, a work environment, or a potential market necessitates different approaches. It is a generally known fact that characters, organizational cultures, and country customs vary. So, look before you leap.
- Life happens at a continuously increasing speed, as we grow older. Perceived from a bright angle it means that at our old age we should never be bored, because the given fact of our decelerated motions and minds combined with the amount of life we will then have behind us, will make a day as short as a minute.
- Contentment should be considered the highest achievement in life: it is the break that the soul needs to reenergize for future encounters with turbulence. It's the deep breath that we take when we are in full nature, and we feel that our lungs need fresh air. It's the essence of life and the decisive factor between giving up and persevering. It's the rebirth of hope. Yes: Contentment is the reward we get when we decide to choose for ourselves . . . above all.
- Failure is just an opinion. In the first place in the eyes of the one who experiences it. It hurts. It makes you feel unworthy. It makes you wonder about yourself. But it also creates the possibility for you to get to know yourself better . . . if you allow that.
- Beware of forgetfulness once you've realized your dreams! There are so many things that are actually obvious, but still remain unpracticed, or are ceased to be done, because people get in some kind of daze when they acquire certain positions. The good intentions end when the dreams come true . . .
- Everybody has flaws. Even the so-called great ones were not without shortcomings: Lincoln wasn't, Martin Luther King wasn't, and JFK wasn't. Yet, these great ones still deserve to be respected, as they were put on earth to serve a purpose: They were the instruments to realize the predestined course of history. If they had never lived, someone else would have played their role. It's as simple as that.
- Choosing is not always easy. Every choice you make has an equal chance to turn out right or wrong: it all depends on your actions AFTER you made the choice. And much of those actions depend on your personality and the value of the underlying subject to you. This may explain why some people refrain from making choices. Some chances are not worth being taken: some sacrifices are not worth being made: some prices are not worth being paid. Peace of mind may lay in . . . not making a choice at all . . .

- Living is the one requirement for all of us without which nothing else is possible. If you want to be a good leader for yourself and others, you should realize that the art of living lies in a good balance in everything you do: enough hard work, enough exercise, enough fun, and enough rest. You just perform better when you are in balance. Remember: you exude what you are, whether you are aware of it or not.

Listen. Listen with your ears. Listen with your eyes. Listen with your mind. Listen with your heart. Listen to the spoken words. Listen to the unspoken ones too. Bring all these ways of listening in one harmonious entirety, and you are the exemplification of a leader.

48

ABOUT MAKING CHOICES

One of the reasons why leadership remains a fascinating topic is because it has so many dimensions and layers, and encompasses an immense range of perceptions. What one considers leadership, another may not agree with. What one considers a perfect leadership skill, another may disregard as unfitting in the leadership scope. Yet, there are some actions and skills that are generally agreed upon as being important in leadership. Some of these are vision, communication skills, understanding, knowledge, and determination.

An aspect that is as critical to leadership as the ones mentioned previously is choice. Leaders make choices all the time, and they understand that every choice holds a degree of risk, because there are always factors that are not known or cannot be foreseen when making choices. And yet: choices are foundational in leading. In order to clarify this, let's take a step back, and consider the way we define leadership here. Some people see leadership as an act that involves a leader, followers, and a situation. Here, however, as indicated at several stages in this book, leadership starts at an earlier stage: before followers or "others" are involved. Facing different situations, we have to make decisions, and whenever that happens, we are engaging in leadership, with or without others included. Call it self-leadership, if you wish to distinguish between the traditional interpretation and this one, but it's leadership nonetheless.

Decision-making entails choices. In order to make a decision, we weigh alternatives and select one option. That's a choice. Our life is filled with choices, and not only simple ones such as what clothes we will put on today, or whether we will take the bus, bike, or train to work. Who and what we are today is largely based on the choices we made in the past. Where we will be in the future is also largely dependent upon the choices we make today. Leaders are particularly aware of that. Choices are not always easy to make. They require skills that we often take for granted, but that can enhance the quality of the choices we make. Some of these skills are:

- Mindfulness: This refers to our ability to be aware of all the factors that matter in the choice process. In making choices, especially those with high impact, there is no room for neglecting factors that could be critical for the outcome. We will therefore have to be attentive to details, but also to the bigger picture.
- Reflection: Oftentimes, when we are facing choices, we have to tap from past experiences, but also use our imagination to envision possible outcomes. This reflective process can help us eliminate some choices that may seem appealing, but could carry consequences we may not want to deal with.
- Courage: No matter how much information we have at hand; there will always be unknown factors. Every choice is therefore a courageous act: a leap in the dark, which may require smart adjustments when complications arise that we had not foreseen.
- Intelligence: Some choices require intellectual intelligence, such as knowledge, design thinking, and strategic insight; while others ask for emotional intelligence, including empathy and deep listening. This often depends on the nature of the choice and who or what is involved.
- Consideration: While reflection and intelligence do a decent job in getting to the choice to be made, it is a consideration that can be seen as the final aspect. Consideration is the process of weighing all the options, just before making a decision.

In spite of its importance in the leadership process, choice is not often listed as a leadership skill. It is one of those qualities we take for granted, just like our breath, because we have all have made choices for the longest time in our lives. But choices can lead to wonderful or disastrous outcomes. It is therefore equally important for leaders to know, that the choice is highly important, but the action implemented *after* a choice has been made, underscore the ability of a leader to think creatively, show perseverance, and remain balanced.

A specific aspect to consider when you need to make a choice, especially if it's an impactful one, is time. Your best chances of making proper choices and obtaining a better mental balance overall—choices or not—lie in making a conscious time donation to yourself. I call this the wealthiest moment of the day. The wealthiest moment in a day is the moment that you allow yourself to sit for a while in a peaceful environment; in a comfortable position; and let your mind flow.

The more spiritually oriented ones among us may refer to such a moment as meditation, but it does not necessarily have to be that, for meditation is usually described as a state in which you are thoughtless, focusing on one single point while banning all concerns, plans, dreams, emotions, and other activities from your brain, although a more experienced meditator will probably develop the ability to meditate even under less convenient circumstances.

However, the moment of wealth I am alluding to here is one that is achievable for everyone: busy corporate executives, devoted house makers, talented artists, drifting souls, you name it. It merely entails taking a moment to enjoy serenity: sounds off, lights dim, temperature pleasant, and seating comfortable. And although your mind may be racing a mile a minute at the start, you will gradually feel a sense of tranquility embracing you as you engage more into the peacefulness of the moment: you may experience an increased acceptance of life as it is presented to you; an understanding of the possible reasons for your experiences; and a contentment with where you are now.

The difference between such a wealthy moment and the traditional description of meditation may also be explained as such: In your wealthy moment it is perfectly normal, and even expected, that you will think and remain aware of everything around you, whereas meditation predominantly relates to emptying yourself for a little while in order to enhance your future capacity to cope with matters.

As you may consequently conclude, the moment of wealth does not require any previous exercise: no elevated spiritual awareness or secluded lifestyle. On the contrary: it is the perfect way for busy socializers to spend some time alone and to refocus by sorting out their thoughts.

Yet, you should avoid taking your moment of wealth when you are in the thick of your workday unless you can find a peaceful place right in the heart of everything and create the earlier mentioned atmosphere: no immediate sound, dimmed lights, pleasant temperature, and easy seating.

The moment of wealth should nonetheless not be underestimated as it may bring about ingenuity in managing daily problems of a kind that you might have been incapable of if you just kept pressing yourself without a pause: Thinking is a healthy, prominent, and rewarding activity, especially when done in an atmosphere of tranquility. It may transform you into a less impulsive, more responsible action taker. It is therefore no frivolous advice to try practicing this moment if you never did before, regardless of the enormity of your current responsibilities, projects, or emotional pressures. The wealthiest moment of your day, whether it lasts 15 minutes or an hour, may not immediately lead to solutions for your concerns but it will help you perceive things in their relativity: oversee the forest that is your current life and arrange your issues according to importance. Most of all, it will bring you in closer connection with—and fill you with greater respect for—the one that will always stick by you: yourself.

49

LETTING THE GENIE OUT OF THE BOTTLE

IMPERMANENCE

Behind us
lie millions of lives—
converted to history
in fading shades of gray.
Great or unwieldy—
that no longer matters.
They led to this moment
that's now slipping away.

~ *Joan Marques*

As you may have picked up by now, this book focuses on developing and nurturing awakened leadership practices, with the aim to assist you in being the best leader you can be, to yourself as well as to others.

Awakened leadership, which was also described in the introductory section of this book, could be labeled as one of several "new-age" leadership styles, born out of frustration with the self-centered, greed-based, mindless leadership actions of past decades, or it can be considered an entire way of being.

Regardless of how you decide to look at it, it remains a highly useful way of dealing with the responsibility of leadership in any setting, whether private or professional; small, mid-sized, or large scaled, or whether pertaining to the self or others. So, what is so useful about it? The main reason is this: Awakened leadership is reflective. When you reflect on things, you consider them from multiple angles, and think deeper about them than a superficial thought or two. Your job, position, work relationships, the industry you are involved in, the very purpose of your performance, your private or social connections, the things you say, the things you do, and those you refrain from saying and doing: reflecting on all of the above can help you understand yourself better, and make you more mindful from here onward.

One of the greatest favors you can do yourself is understanding why you do what you do, and who is affected by your actions. Especially when you are about to make major decisions, such as laying off a number of employees, discontinuing or starting a new production or service line, engaging in a new relationship or terminating an old one, it may be helpful if you write down the perceived impact. When considering important steps, we often underestimate the number of stakeholders whose lives will be influenced by these steps. Take a few minutes and start writing. The group of affected parties is usually five times higher than what your initial thoughts may have wanted you to believe.

As also mentioned before in this book, awakened leadership is the opposite of sleepwalking leadership. First: What is sleepwalking leadership? It is the trend of making decisions without considering that:

1. Everything changes and nothing is today as it was yesterday, so you cannot continue to make the same decisions you made yesterday hoping they will have the same outcomes.
2. "Reality," as you see it, is not the same as how others see it. Your reality is shaped by a number of influencing factors, such as your upbringing, culture, character, generation, education, values, and more. You can therefore not consider that others will always understand and appreciate your perspectives.
3. Traditional patterns or habits are the most common ways of driving you into the autopilot state, thus, sleepwalking mode: You follow these patterns or apply these habits without thinking, and definitely, without reflecting if they still make sense in your life as it is today. Mindlessly submitting to recurring patterns or habits makes us followers, not leaders.
4. Focusing too much on the details can make you lose sight of the bigger purpose of something. Some people can get so lost in the details that these become the main goal of their performance, causing them to entirely lose track of the larger scheme of things.
5. Mindless leadership has maneuvered us into a global ecological crisis, and every plan, step, decision, or action you undertake from now on—individually or collectively—will either be instrumental to a positive turnaround, or will further augment the problems we, the human species, have created in the past century.

With the above stipulated, awakened leadership can easily be understood, through the following behavioral roadmap. Awakened leadership is the continued awareness in your thoughts, actions, and communications that:

1. You have to make your decisions by reflecting on your lessons learned from past experiences, but even more by reflection on your wishes for the future and the possible effects these decisions will have on that.

2. You should consider the perspectives of others, and keep an open mind to potentially different ideas, which as they may enrich your understanding, insight, and consequently, the directions you will choose going forward.

3. You should question, even doubt, established patterns and procedures, as many of them were created when times, expectations, circumstances, goals, and mindsets, were entirely different. If you find that the old patterns and procedures still suffice, you can continue with them, but if you find that there is room for improvement or drastic change, you should implement that.

4. You should keep in mind that, while details are important to safeguard quality in everything, you also have to keep the big picture in mind, so that you can focus on what really matters in the long run.

5. You should make mindful leadership your new habit. Your mind is a wonderful instrument, but it has the tendency to lead you astray at every opportunity it gets. This is the time to step up in awareness and regain control over the directions your mind moves into.

Restore your priorities in the right order, and realize the impermanence of everything, including yourself. If you can keep yourself mindful of the fact that you want to leave this world a better place than you encountered it, you have set an important step on the path to awakened leadership.

50

ON TREADING THE NOBLE EIGHTFOLD PATH

(A Splash of Buddhist Psychology)

Buddhist psychology (not to be confused with religion) has made important advances into the behavioral chronicles of both Western and non-Western thinkers in the past century and continues to do so today. There are many reasons for this advancement, one being the need for more engaged leadership. Today's workforce yearns for leaders that believe in philanthropy and elevate their minds and actions beyond self-interest (Kemavuthanon & Duberley, 2009).

Buddhism has been around for more than 2,500 years. The man we came to know as "the Buddha" was named Gautama Siddhartha, and lived from about 563 or 566 BCE to about 486 BCE. Siddhartha, who was the son of a tribal king, distanced himself from his affluent background as a young man, and subsequently acquired some valuable insights over the course of his life. The Buddha's insights have been formalized in various "vehicles" or "schools," were passed on through the centuries, and have since spread worldwide. The most commonly known schools, sometimes referred to as "vehicles," are Theravada, also known as the older, smaller vehicle, and Mahayana, also known as the larger vehicle. Even though they have some important philosophical differences, the two schools share a number of critical foundational insights and teachings such as suffering, impermanence, no-self, karma, nirvana, dependent origination, mindfulness, and the Four Noble Truths and the Noble Eightfold Path (Marques, 2015).

Buddhism presents a specific worldview and way of living that leads to personal understanding, happiness, and a wholesome development (Johansen & Gopalakrishna, 2006). The Buddha is not to be worshipped as a god but revered as an awakened teacher.

The Four Noble Truths

The Four Noble Truths were defined by the Buddha and became foundational in his post-enlightenment lectures. The Four Noble Truths are, in fact, a sequence of insights:

1. The truth of suffering (suffering exists).
2. The truth of the origin of suffering (suffering has a cause).
3. The truth of the cessation of suffering (suffering can be ended).
4. The truth of the path, the way to liberation from suffering (the path to end suffering).

Suffering is, in this context, actually an insufficient term, because the Buddha intended to encompass much more with the word that he used, which was "Dukkha." Dukkha pertains to more than suffering, pain, or misery. It suggests the foundational unsatisfactory sense we get from existing. It refers to the lack of perfection and the constant struggle and strives that are associated with life (Bodhi, N/A).

The First Noble Truth establishes the foundation of reality: suffering exists. In this regard, "suffering" pertains life as a whole, and the many instances of anguish it brings, from birth to death, from illness to aging, and from unpleasant experiences to the inability to obtain or hold on to the things we crave (Trungpa, 2009).

The Second Noble Truth, which states that suffering has a cause, can be easily understood once we have obtained an understanding of what the First Noble Truth entails. This Second Noble Truth encompasses the reality of gaining things and losing them again: the recurring manifestations of impermanence, which can cause mourning and oftentimes even a sense of devastation. Because human beings are possessive by nature, we have a drive to obtain and cherish, and the fact that we can only hold anything, even our youth, our health, our loved ones, and even our life, for only a while, causes suffering (Rahula, 1974). We have a tendency to cling to people, places, experiences, wishes, ideas, or mindsets, and this causes suffering (Nyanatiloka, 1970).

The Third Noble Truth, suffering can be ended, shines a positive light on the grimness that emanates from the first two: it is possible to become free from suffering. In order to attain this, however, the cause of our suffering has to be terminated, which means that desires and aversions will have to be annihilated. Rahula (1974) describes the state of having released our desires, thus having ended our suffering, as the attainment of nirvana.

The Four Noble Truths can be seen as the essence of the Buddha's teaching (Bodhi, N/A). The first three Noble Truths, as explained previously, are intended as points of understanding, and the fourth, which entails the Noble Eightfold Path, as a practice to be implemented if one chooses to address the issue of suffering. A good way of looking at it is, that the First Truth has to be understood, the

Second Truth has to be abandoned, the Third Truth has to be realized, and the Fourth Truth has to be developed (Bodhi, N/A).

The Noble Eightfold Path

The Fourth Noble Truth provides an actual way to end suffering: The Noble Eightfold Path. This Path encompasses the following practices or insights: Right View; Right Intention; Right Speech; Right Action; Right Livelihood; Right Effort; Right Mindfulness; and Right Concentration. There is no specific sequence in this set of insights, because they are interrelated. However, it might be prudent to start the review of this path with right view for the simple reason that right view enhances the understanding of the first three Noble Truths, while it also augments insight into the importance of these interconnected elements of the Path. In other words, it links the awareness of the initial three Noble Truths to the contents of the Fourth. Yet, that is just one way of perceiving "right view." In fact, the entire scope of the Four Noble Truths and the Noble Eightfold Path can be reduced to two essentials, 1, Suffering, and 2, The end of suffering (Gethin, 1998).

When considering the path, it becomes clear that each part is integrated and can serve as a good preparation to the next. For instance, right mindfulness, which can be attained through meditation, leads to the right concentration (Gombrich, 1988). In the following section, we will engage in a brief contemplation of each tread of the path and bring this within the realm of leadership, thus attempting to demonstrate how this tread could benefit leaders.

The Noble Eightfold Path as Leadership Compass

Right view. Right view is as good a starting point of the path as any of the other elements. Right view entails our ability to detect which of our mindsets are constructive and nourish those. It also influences our perception: the way we consider things that happen to and around us. We have the ability to either maintain a negative view and perceive everything as an attack to the quality of life or consider matters from a positive angle and distinguish the positive lessons in each experience. Right view adjusts limiting perspectives, and may even lead us to understand that actually, all perspectives are limiting. Thus, right view influences our attitude.

Right intention. Right intention, also referred to as "right thinking," pertains to mental focus. Maintaining a right intention is not as easy as it may seem. Thich (1998) recommends four actions to refrain from losing right intention: (1) ensuring proper understanding of what we see, read or hear, and contemplate on things first, since first impressions may be misleading; (2) scrutinizing our actions in order to verify that we are not mindlessly exerting adopted habits, but engage in well-considered behavior; (3) inspecting our habits, and acknowledging that we have good and bad ones. Knowing our bad habits can help us refrain from allowing them to emerge at times when we least need them; and (4) nurturing an awakened mind in order to benefit others as much as possible. In Buddhism, this is referred to as "Bodhicitta." When we engage in Bodhicitta, we become filled with the intention to do well onto others and help them become happier beings.

Right speech. These times of massive, multiple communication avenues have brought the importance of right speech more to the forefront than ever before. Words are critical vehicles of information sharing, and they can be either constructive or destructive. Engaging in right speech entails deliberate refraining from saying things that negatively affect others. It further entails practicing mindfulness when sharing information that has not been verified and could be harmful to other parties. Right speech means telling the truth to the best of your abilities, not creating divisiveness by telling different people different things, refraining from making cruel statements, and refraining from overstatements (Thich, 1998).

Right livelihood. This pertains to the ways people earn their living. It predominantly focuses on the nature of the work one does, and whether this is constructive or not. Thich (1998) suggests some of the critical questions one could reflect on to ensure right livelihood, such as (a) whether one is producing, dealing in, or promoting weapons of any kind that are being used to kill and destroy; (b) whether one is engaging in practices where people are blatantly being taken advantage of, or (c) whether one is involved in the production and/or promotion of destructive products such as alcohol and drugs.

Right effort. Also listed as "right diligence," right effort is a very deliberate act. While effort is generally an admirable practice, it can be directed to constructive or destructive activities. People who work in industries that produce items for destruction undeniably invest effort in their job. Unfortunately, this cannot be considered right effort, due to the suffering it causes. Right effort, like all other treads of the eightfold path, requires careful evaluation of our actions, thoughts, and intentions, in order to assess whether they are constructive. Similar to the other elements of the path, right effort is very personal in nature as well. It should be applied as a way of contemplating on the roots of our suffering, and subsequently engaging in the effort to release those roots.

Right mindfulness. In practicing mindfulness we also practice all other facets of the eightfold path: right view, right intention, right speech, right action, right livelihood, right effort, and right concentration. When we are mindful, we see things that we usually take for granted: the grass, the trees, our partner, our colleagues, our pet, and we realize fully that they are here now. It is our mindfulness that can guide us toward truly appreciating what we see, and displaying our gratitude for their presence. Through our mindfulness, we may instigate the mindfulness of others. The appreciation that is part of mindfulness can alleviate the suffering of mindlessness, and encourage us to go a step further, so that we concentrate on others, understand them better, and transform our own suffering and theirs into joy (Thich, 1998).

Right concentration. Right concentration is firmly intertwined with the other elements of the Noble Eightfold Path. Right concentration is oftentimes also referred to as Right meditation. Right mindfulness and concentration are both tools to sharpen the mind (Nouri, 2013), and can both be amplified through mindfulness meditation, also known as Vipassana. Concentration is required to be present wherever we are. Once we can attain that, we enjoy each moment to the fullest, and cease our excessive concerns about the past or the future. Through right concentration, we can discover beautiful scenes that used to escape us when we were not concentrating. Right concentration can therefore lead us to greater happiness, since we are more focused on what matters now. If we engage deep enough in right concentration, we will ultimately start realizing the impermanent nature of many of our cravings and learn to release them (Thich, 1998).

A Mindful Moral Compass for 21st-Century Leadership

The conclusive section of this chapter consists of an urgent request to you, who understands the importance of a primarily sustainability and life-cherishing oriented leadership style toward the future. This is the time to shift our paradigms from growth prioritization to a focus on cultivation of life-sustaining resources. Profits are an important strategy for corporate evolution, but in our day and age, another evolution requires more attention: the evolution of life and therewith, the safeguarding and restoration of critical resources, along with a focus on initiatives and actions that promote a better quality of life for all occupants of planet earth. Leaders who withstand the temptation of short-term returns, and who dare to engage in activities that aim to achieve a better quality of life for all will experience greater support, witness more growth, and find more gratification in their practices than those who continue to cling to an obsolete paradigm.

A critical point to underscore once again here is the fact that the elements of the Noble Eightfold Path are interrelated and inspire one another. An interpretation of implementing the Noble Eightfold Path could thus be as follows: a leader who engages in (morally) right *view* will *mindfully concentrate* on decisions that are based on the improvement of the quality of life for all stakeholders. Consequently, all *intention*, communication (*speech*), *effort*, and *actions* of this leader will be geared toward the goal of behaving morally sound. With such a mindful approach from initial views to ultimate actions, the leader becomes aware of the need to engage in right *livelihood*, as (s)he consistently gauges his or her accomplishments to the high moral standards developed.

References

Bodhi, B. (N/A). The four noble truths. Retrieved February 6, 2016, from www.beyond thenet.net/dhamma/fourNoble.htm.

Gethin, R. (1998). *The Foundations of Buddhism.* Oxford University Press, Oxford.

Gombrich, R. F. (1988). *Theravada Buddhism: A Social History From Ancient Benares to Modern Colombo*. Routledge and Kegan Paul, London.

Johansen, B. C., & Gopalakrishna, D. (2006). A Buddhist view of adult learning in the workplace. *Advances in Developing Human Resources*, *8*(3), pp. 337–345.

Kemavuthanon, S., & Duberley, J. (2009). A Buddhist view of leadership: The case of the OTOP project. *Leadership & Organization Development Journal*, *30*(8), pp. 737–758.

Marques, J. (2015). *Business and Buddhism*. Routledge, New York, NY.

Nouri, D. (May 3, 2013). What is the eightfold path? Secular Buddhist Association. Retrieved April 1, 2016, from http://secularbuddhism.org/2013/05/03/what-is-the-eightfold-path/.

Nyanatiloka, T. (1970). *Buddhist Dictionary: Manual of Buddhist Terms and Doctrines* (T. Nyanaponika, Ed., 3rd Rev. ed.). Buddhist Publication Society, Kandy, Sri Lanka.

Rahula, W. (1974). *The Heritage of the Bhikkhu: The Buddhist Tradition of Service*. Grove Press, New York, NY.

Thich, N. H. (1998). *The Heart of the Buddha's Teaching: Transforming Suffering Into Peace, Joy, and Liberation*. Broadway Books, New York, NY.

Trungpa, Y. (2009). *The Truth of Suffering and the Path of Liberation* (J. Lief, Ed.). Shambala Publications, Boston, MA.

51
MOVING FORWARD FROM HERE

RETROSPECT

The old up and down
Sometimes brings me a frown
Today, everything seems great
Tomorrow brings a twist of fate
It's an ever-swinging carrousel
That, by now, I should know well
Yet, life remains a big surprise
And maybe that's its very spice

We find ourselves moving from boom
To insecure and pitch-black doom
What keeps us hanging on this slope
Is our steady, incorrigible hope
That, even though today we whine
Tomorrow again the sun will shine
And what today may seem like night
Will transform into promising light

People come and people go
Today a friend, tomorrow foe
Positions, minds and visions change
What's normal now, was once so strange

> The person that I am today
> Doesn't resemble the old me in any way
> So, on I bounce, between joy and sorrow
> Here today, and gone tomorrow.
>
> ~ *Joan Marques*

The days in which we currently live are challenging in many ways: aside from a mind-boggling, nerve-racking pandemic and a long overdue movement for social justice, we realize that change happens at a continuous and dazzling speed. Professions on which society was built for the longest time are disappearing, the job market is incessantly shifting with many opportunities moving to other parts of the world, and learning in itself has never been a more ambiguous process, because the future is unpredictable, so you can't possible know what you are really preparing yourself for.

And yet, these are days of great opportunities. Whatever you want to know is basically at your fingertips. Those of us who are older remember the pre-internet days, when knowledge had to be obtained from brick-and-mortar libraries, newspapers and news shows, or expensive encyclopedias. Everything was therefore limited to time, accessibility, and means. Nothing was as instantaneous as it is today. It took quite some effort to get to the source of any piece of information needed. The ease with which we can currently access global databases, news sources, or simply obtain answers to general—or specific—questions is astounding, even though it has become the new "normal," making very few people reflect on the blessing captured in this status quo.

If you have any kind of talent, you don't need a whole lot of funds or connections with powerful people to display what you can: the social networks offer plentiful opportunities to share your skills, and many of today's successes found their initial push through the net.

Being an introvert is no longer a barrier to meeting people and establishing rewarding connections. Great friendships and wonderful long-term relationships— even marriages—were established and cultivated through the same medium that was responsible for the two previously mentioned advantages, the internet.

Borders are no longer barriers because people now continuously communicate with one another through numerous venues at thousands of miles' distance as if they were sitting right beside each other. Costs are also a disappearing barrier because internet and telephone connections have seen their most expensive days. We are heading toward a world without borders, and with that, one with greater mutual acceptance and understanding.

Dreaming has never been as attractive as it is today because the chance to realize your dreams has never been so abundantly present. So, why would the turnaround of people's lives be limited to unknown individuals? More than ever, we all have it in our hands to determine who and what we want to be.

With knowledge, relationships, insights, and exploratory tools within arms' reach, we really have little or no excuse to be left behind. The only thing we need from ourselves is willpower and courage. Those qualities are not for sale, and cannot be taught per se. But they can be mustered and cultivated because we all have them in our system.

With all the opportunities within reach, staying behind has practically become a non-option. So, what are your plans?

INDEX

Printed in the United States
by Baker & Taylor Publisher Services